Pro·Lighting

GLAMOUR SHOTS

Pro·Lighting

ROGER HICKS and FRANCES SCHULTZ

GLAMOUR
SHOTS

ROTOVISION

A Quarto Book

Published and distributed by ROTOVISION SA
Route Suisse 9
CH-1295 Mies
Switzerland
Tel: +41 (22) 755 30 55
Fax: +41 (22) 755 40 72

Distributed to the trade in the United States:
Watson-Guptill Publications
1515 Broadway
New York, NY 10036

ISBN 2-88046-229-0

This book was designed and produced by
Quarto Publishing plc
6 Blundell Street
London N7 9BH

Creative Director: Richard Dewing
Designer: Mark Roberts
Editor: Sue Thraves
Project Editor: Anna Briffa
Picture Researchers: Roger Hicks and Frances Schultz

Typeset in Great Britain by
Central Southern Typesetters, Eastbourne
Printed in Singapore by Teck Wah Paper Products Ltd.
Production and Separation in Singapore by ProVision Pte. Ltd.
Tel: +65 334 7720
Fax: +65 334 7721

CONTENTS

▼

▼

THE MOST COMMON RESPONSE FROM THE PHOTOGRAPHERS WHO CONTRIBUTED TO THIS BOOK, WHEN THE CONCEPT WAS EXPLAINED TO THEM, WAS "I'D BUY THAT". THE AIM IS SIMPLE: TO CREATE A LIBRARY OF BOOKS, ILLUSTRATED WITH FIRST-CLASS PHOTOGRAPHY FROM ALL AROUND THE WORLD, WHICH SHOW EXACTLY HOW EACH INDIVIDUAL PHOTOGRAPH IN EACH BOOK WAS LIT.

Who will find it useful? Professional photographers, obviously, who are either working in a given field or want to move into a new field. Students, too, who will find that it gives them access to a much greater range of ideas and inspiration than even the best college can hope to present. Art directors and others in the visual arts will find it a useful reference book, both for ideas and as a means of explaining to photographers exactly what they want done. It will also help them to understand what the photographers are saying to them. Finally, of course, "pro/am" photographers who are on the cusp between amateur photography and earning money with their cameras will find it invaluable: it shows both the standards that are required, and the means of achieving them.

The lighting set-ups in each book vary widely, and embrace many different types of light source: electronic flash, tungsten, HMIs, and light brushes, sometimes mixed with daylight and flames and all kinds of other things. Some are very complex, while others are very simple. This variety is important, both as a source of ideas and inspiration and because each book as a whole has no axe to grind: there is no editorial bias towards one kind of lighting or another, because the pictures were chosen on the basis of impact and occasionally on the basis of technical difficulty. Certain subjects are, after all, notoriously difficult to light and can present a challenge even to experienced photographers. Only after the picture selection has been made was there any attempt to understand the lighting set-up.

While the books were being put together, it was however interesting to

see how there was often a broad consensus of opinion on equipment and techniques within a particular discipline. In food photography for example, one might correctly have predicted that most

photographers would use cool-running flash rather than hot tungsten, which melts ice-cream and dries out moist food; but the remarkable prevalence of slight back lighting might not have been so immediately obvious to anyone not

experienced in that field. In glamour, there was much more use of tungsten – perhaps to keep the model warm? – but a surprising number of photographers shot daylight film under tungsten lighting for a seriously warm effect. After going through each book, one can very nearly devise a "universal lighting set-up" which will work for the majority of pictures in a particular speciality, and which needs only to be tinkered with to suit individual requirements. One will also see that there are many other ways of doing things.

The structure of the books is straightforward. After this initial introduction, which is common to all the books in the series, there is a brief guide and glossary of lighting terms. Then, there is a specific introduction to the individual area or areas of photography which are covered by the book. Sub-divisions of each discipline are arranged in chapters, inevitably with a degree of overlap, and each chapter has its own introduction. Finally, at the end of the book, there is a directory of those photographers who have contributed work.

If you would like your work to be considered for inclusion in future books, please write to Quarto Publishing plc, 6 Blundell Street, London N7 9BH, England, and request an Information Pack. DO NOT SEND PICTURES, either with the initial inquiry or with any subsequent correspondence, unless requested; unsolicited pictures may not always be returned. When a book is planned which corresponds with your particular area of expertise, we will contact you. Until then, we hope that you enjoy this book, that you find it useful, and that it helps you in your work.

▼

THE LIGHTING DRAWINGS IN THIS BOOK WERE PREPARED FROM SKETCHES SUPPLIED BY THE PHOTOGRAPHERS THEMSELVES. NEEDLESS TO SAY, THESE VARIED SOMEWHAT IN QUALITY AND IN THE CARE WITH WHICH THEY WERE PUT TOGETHER. THEY HAVE HOWEVER BEEN CHECKED AGAINST THE PICTURES BY AN EXPERIENCED INDEPENDENT PHOTOGRAPHER, AND WHERE THERE WERE DISCREPANCIES, WE HOPE THAT THEY HAVE ALL BEEN CLARIFIED.

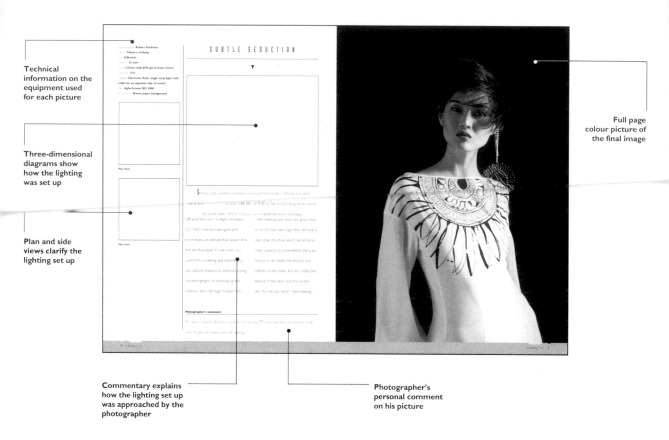

Technical information on the equipment used for each picture

Three-dimensional diagrams show how the lighting was set up

Plan and side views clarify the lighting set up

Commentary explains how the lighting set up was approached by the photographer

Photographer's personal comment on his picture

Full page colour picture of the final image

The drawings are not necessarily to scale, but that does not matter. After all, no photographer works strictly according to rules and preconceptions: there is always room to move this light a little to the left or right, to move that light closer or further away, and so forth. Likewise, the precise power of the individual lighting heads, or more importantly the lighting ratios are not always given; but again, this is something which can be "fine tuned" by the photographer if he or she wishes to reproduce the lighting set-ups in here. Besides, flash heads vary widely in efficiency, and therefore in light output

for a given rated power, and reflectors also vary widely in efficiency. In any case, people cannot always remember the finer details of what they did: lights are moved this way and that, or their power turned up or down, in accordance with the needs of the shot, and no records are kept.

We are however confident that there is more than enough information given about every single shot to merit its inclusion in the book: as well as just lighting techniques, there are also all kinds of hints and tips about commercial realities, photographic practicalities, and

the way of the world in general.

The book can therefore be used in a number of ways. The most basic, and perhaps the most useful for the beginner, is to study all the technical information concerning a picture which he or she particularly admires, together with the lighting diagrams, and to try to duplicate that shot as far as possible with the equipment available. We have deliberately omitted information about which makes of camera and lens were used, because it really does not matter very much whether you use a Linhof or an Arca or a Sinar; the important thing is the format. The same would be true of a Hasselblad or a Mamiya. The same is of course true of the focal length: using a 127mm lens on a 6x7 cm camera is after all much the same as using 110mm or 120mm on 6x6 cm.

A more advanced use for the book is as a problem solver for difficulties you have already encountered: a particular technique of back lighting, say, or of creating a feeling of light and space. And, of course, it can always be used simply as a source of inspiration: "I wonder what would happen if I took *this* technique and applied it to *this* subject . . ."

The information for each picture follows the same plan, though some individual headings may be omitted if they were irrelevant or unavailable. The photographer is credited first, then the client, together with the use for which the picture was taken. Next come the other members of the team who worked on the picture: stylists, models, art directors, or whoever. Camera and lens come next, followed by exposure. Where the lighting is electronic flash, only the aperture is given, as illumination is of course independent of shutter speed. Next, the lighting equipment is briefly summarized – whether tungsten or flash, and what sort of heads – and then comes film. With film, we have named brands and types, because different films have very different ways of rendering colours and tonal values. Finally there is a brief note on props and backgrounds. Often, this last entry will be obvious from the picture, but in other cases you may be surprised at what has been pressed into service, and how different it looks from its normal role.

However the most important part of the book is the pictures themselves. By studying these, and referring to the lighting diagrams and the text as necessary, you can work out how they were done; and showing how things are done is the brief to which the *Pro Lighting* series was created.

DIAGRAM KEY

The following is a key to the symbols used in the three-dimensional and plan view diagrams. All commonly used elements such as standard heads, reflectors etc., are listed. Any special or unusual elements involved will be shown on the relevant diagrams themselves.

THREE-DIMENSIONAL DIAGRAMS

large format camera   medium format camera   35 mm camera

standard head   standard head with barn doors   spot

strip   soft box   light brush

reflector/diffuser/flag   backdrop   table

PLAN VIEW DIAGRAMS

large format camera   medium format camera   35 mm camera   flag

standard head   standard head with barn doors   spot   cookie

diffuser

reflector

strip   soft box   light brush   backdrop   table

GLOSSARY OF LIGHTING TERMS

▼

LIGHTING, LIKE ANY OTHER CRAFT, HAS ITS OWN JARGON AND SLANG. UNFORTUNATELY, THE DIFFERENT TERMS ARE NOT VERY WELL STANDARDIZED, AND OFTEN THE SAME THING MAY BE DESCRIBED IN TWO OR MORE WAYS OR THE SAME WORD MAY BE USED TO MEAN TWO OR MORE DIFFERENT THINGS. FOR EXAMPLE, A SHEET OF BLACK CARD, WOOD, METAL OR OTHER MATERIAL WHICH IS USED TO CONTROL REFLECTIONS OR SHADOWS MAY BE CALLED A FLAG, A FRENCH FLAG, A DONKEY OR A GOBO — THOUGH SOME PEOPLE WOULD RESERVE THE TERM "GOBO" FOR A FLAG WITH HOLES IN IT, WHICH IS ALSO KNOWN AS A COOKIE. IN THIS BOOK, WE HAVE TRIED TO STANDARDIZE TERMS AS FAR AS POSSIBLE. FOR CLARITY, A GLOSSARY IS GIVEN BELOW, AND THE PREFERRED TERMS USED IN THIS BOOK ARE ASTERISKED.

Acetate
see Gel

Acrylic sheeting
Hard, shiny plastic sheeting, usually methyl methacrylate, used as a diffuser ("opal") or in a range of colours as a background.

*Barn doors
Adjustable flaps affixed to a lighting head which allow the light to be shaded from a particular part of the subject.

Barn doors

Boom
Extension arm allowing a light to be cantilevered out over a subject.

*Bounce
A passive reflector, typically white but also, for example, silver or gold, from which light is bounced back onto the subject. Also used in the compound term "Black Bounce", meaning a flag used to absorb light rather than to cast a shadow.

Continuous lighting
What its name suggests: light which shines continuously instead of being a brief flash.

Contrast
see Lighting ratio

Cookie
see Gobo

*Diffuser
Translucent material used to diffuse light. Includes tracing paper, scrim, umbrellas, translucent plastics such as Perspex and Plexiglas, and more.

Electronic flash: standard head with parallel snoot (Strobex)

Donkey
see Gobo

Effects light
Neither key nor fill; a small light, usually a spot, used to light a particular part of the subject. A hair light on a model is an example of an effects (or "FX") light.

*Fill
Extra lights, either from a separate head or from a reflector, which "fills" the shadows and lowers the lighting ratio.

Fish fryer
A small Soft Box.

*Flag
A rigid sheet of metal, board, foam-core or other material which is used to absorb light or to create a shadow. Many flags are painted black on one side and white (or brushed silver) on the other, so that they can be used either as flags or as reflectors.

*Flat
A large Bounce, often made of a thick sheet of expanded polystyrene or foam-core (for lightness).

Foil
see Gel

French flag
see Flag

Frost
see Diffuser

*Gel
Transparent or sometimes translucent coloured material used to modify the colour of a light. It is an abbreviation of "gelatine (filter)", though most modern "gels" for lighting use are actually of acetate.

*Gobo
As used in this book, synonymous with "cookie": a flag with cut-outs in it, to cast interestingly-shaped shadows. Also used in projection spots.

"Cookies" or "gobos" for projection spotlight (Photon Beard)

*Head
Light source, whether continuous or flash. A "standard head" is fitted with a plain reflector.

*HMI
Rapidly-pulsed and

effectively continuous light source approximating to daylight and running far cooler than tungsten. Relatively new at the time of writing, and still very expensive.

*Honeycomb
Grid of open-ended hexagonal cells, closely resembling a honeycomb. Increases directionality of

Honeycomb (Hensel)

light from any head.

Incandescent lighting
see Tungsten

Inky dinky
Small tungsten spot.

*Key or key light
The dominant or principal light, the light which casts the shadows.

Kill Spill
Large flat used to block spill.

*Light brush
Light source "piped" through fibre-optic lead. Can be used to add highlights, delete shadows and modify lighting, literally by "painting with light".

Electronic Flash: light brush "pencil" (Hensel)

Electronic Flash: light brush "hose" (Hensel)

Lighting ratio
The ratio of the key to the fill, as measured with an incident light meter. A high lighting ratio (8:1 or above) is very contrasty, especially in colour; a low lighting ratio (4:1 or less) is flatter or softer. A 1:1 lighting ratio is completely even, all over the subject.

*Mirror
Exactly what its name suggests. The only reason for mentioning it here is that reflectors are rarely mirrors, because mirrors create "hot spots" while reflectors diffuse light. Mirrors (especially small shaving mirrors) are however widely used, almost in the same way as effects lights.

Nigger
Flag used to shade a background. To "nigger" is to shade from light to dark. The term is no longer used in polite society.

Northlight or North Light
see Soft Box

Perspex
Brand name for acrylic sheeting.

Plexiglas
Brand name for acrylic sheeting.

*Projection spot
Flash or tungsten head with projection optics for casting a clear image of a

gobo or cookie. Used to create textured lighting effects and shadows.

Electronic Flash: projection spotlight (Strobex)

Tungsten Projection spotlight (Photon Beard)

*Reflector
Either a dish-shaped surround to a light, or a bounce.

*Scrim
Heat-resistant fabric diffuser, used to soften lighting.

*Snoot
Conical restrictor, fitting over a lighting head.

The light can only escape from the small hole in the

Tungsten spot with conical snoot (Photon Beard)

Electronic Flash: standard head with parallel snoot (Strobex)

end, and is therefore very directional.

*Soft box
Large, diffuse light source made by shining a light through one or two layers of diffuser. Soft boxes come in all kinds of

Tungsten spot with safety mesh (behind) and wire half diffuser scrim (Photon Beard)

Electronic flash: standard head with large reflector and diffuser (Strobex)

shapes and sizes, from about 30x30cm to 120x180cm and larger. Some soft boxes are rigid; others are made of fabric stiffened with poles resembling fibreglass fishing rods. Also known as a northlight or a windowlight, though these can also be created by shining standard heads through large (120x180cm or larger) diffusers.

*Spill

Light from any source which ends up other than on the subject at which it is pointed. Spill may be used to provide fill, or to light backgrounds, or it may be controlled with flags, barn doors, gobos etc.

*Spot

Directional light source. Normally refers to a light using a focusing system with reflectors or lenses or both, a "focusing spot", but also loosely used as a reflector head rendered more directional with a honeycomb.

*Strip or strip light

Lighting head, usually flash, which is much longer than it is wide.

Electronic flash: strip light with removable barn doors (Strobex)

Strobe

Electronic flash. Strictly, a "strobe" is a stroboscope or rapidly repeating light source, though it is also the name of a leading manufacturer.

Tungsten spot with removable Fresnel lens. The knob at the bottom varies the width of the beam (Photon Beard)

Strobex, formerly Strobe Equipment.

Swimming pool

A very large Soft Box.

*Tungsten

Incandescent lighting. Photographic tungsten

Electronic flash: standard head with standard reflector (Strobex)

lighting runs at 3200°K or 3400°K, as compared with domestic lamps which run at 2400°K to 2800°K or thereabouts.

*Umbrella

Exactly what its name suggests; used for modifying light.

Umbrellas may be used as reflectors (light shining into the umbrella) or diffusers (light shining through the umbrella). The cheapest way of creating a large, soft light source.

Windowlight

Apart from the obvious meaning of light through a window, or of light shone through a diffuser to look as if it is coming through a window, this is another name for a soft box.

Tungsten spot with shoot-through umbrella (Photon Beard)

GLAMOUR SHOTS

▼

Glamour means different things to many people. This is not surprising. All the dictionary definitions of the word seem to turn on magic, illusion and fascination; in other words, on making things seem what they are not. For that matter, we use the word "glamorize" in quite a diffrent way from "glamour". Often, there is a disapproving overtone: a movie director is accused of glamorizing violence, or gangsterism, or whatever. Come to that, in the days before men's magazines turned into journals for the amateur gynaecologist, they used to be known as "glamour" magazines.

Glamour thus wears a Janus face, looking simultaneously forwards and backwards, on light and darkness. This is a major part of its attraction: in seeing what is not normally seen, in revealing what is not normally revealed.

It is a field where it takes a long time to get to the top. By the time you are a successful glamour photographer, you are unlikely to be the young man who first dreamed of being paid to photograph beautiful young women. For that matter, an ever-increasing number of successful glamour photographers are women, who understand better how women want to be seen, and in what context. Years ago, in the heydey of the mens' magazines, everything was much simpler. For the most part, the pictures were fairly straightforward embodiments of average male fantasies, often portrayed with a restraint that was more a result of legal pressures than of good taste. Today, there is really only room at the top: the best photographers, the most beautiful girls, the most exotic locations. The markets are more varied, but more selective: glamour and nude images appear in mainstream magazines and newspapers, and the rules are a lot less repressive. You can show almost anything, heterosexual, homosexual or downright improbable.

Paradoxically, good taste has become more important, not less, because of this freedom. Until comparatively recently, subject matter often took precedence over artistic merit: regardless of the photographer's skill, certain subjects were automatically classified as pornography. Today, the only images which are almost universally banned are those depicting extreme, unsimulated cruelty or the sexual exploitation of children.

Even so, there are wide regional variations. In the United States, for example, nudity is much more problematical than in most of continental Europe, where nudity is not regarded as automatically "wrong" or distasteful. Britain falls somewhere between the two; but in Malta or Singapore for example, where there are two different regimes with two very different cultures, nudity might raise even more problems than in the United States. Another regional variation concerns the definition of "children". In some countries, you are asking for trouble if you photograph a model under the age of 18, unless she is very fully clothed; in others, it is taken for granted that the top models may be in their prime at fifteen or even fourteen, and no one is terribly worried about photographing girls who are even younger.

There are also fashions. Some concern the "look" of the moment: women may be portrayed as slim and ephebian, or as more rounded and traditionally feminine. The old saying that the camera adds five kilos to the model's weight is however certainly true. Fashions in photographing men are more constant; the "he-man", in one form or another, is generally masterful and dominant, though he may be represented as the "mysterious stranger" or as the perfect life companion.

Other fashions concern certain fantasies, and may be more or less strongly regional. "Bondage", at least in a symbolic or cursory form, is an example: at the time of writing, for example, Japan and Germany seem keen on pictures of girls with their hands tied.

THE PURPOSE OF GLAMOUR PHOTOGRAPHY

The vast majority of glamour photographs are of women, so it makes sense to begin with these. It is a truism that women look at pictures of other women, so glamour pictures are not purely to stoke male fantasies or to attract male attention. Even so, different people – and the two sexes – look at glamour pictures in different ways.

At the simplest, it would be a rare man whose attention was not drawn at least momentarily by a picture of a pretty girl. This is why glamour photography is so widely used in advertising, especially in the motor trade; for some reason, motor mechanics and car salesmen are assumed to be peculiarly susceptible to feminine charms. The types of glamour which are used for this sort of photography can however vary widely. Pictures for the motor trade are typically hard-edge and rather raunchy, with a blatant "come-on" in the model's expression; but there are plenty of advertisers who find that a tasteful nude exerts no less powerful an attraction over would-be buyers.

Then again, men who are lonely or in all-male communities like to be reminded what women look like. In these cases, glamour probably reaches its lowest common denominator: the photographs are nothing more or less than the raw material of fantasies.

As for why women look at glamour photography, the most popular theory is that they want to compare themselves with the subjects of the pictures. In some types of advertising, such as lingerie, an element of glamour is all but inevitable; the aim is to persuade the buyer of a particular brand of underwear that she will look desirable, feminine, and so forth. Similar arguments might apply to suntan lotions. In other types of advertising, the theme may be closer to "having it all" — wealth, success, good looks and (by implication) men dancing attendance on you, to be admitted or spurned according to choice. This is very much a power game, and it is one which some women will embrace wholeheartedly; some will reject, equally energetically; and others will treat with more or less open amusement, rejecting it on one level while admitting its charms on another.

PRETTY GIRLS AND BEAUTIFUL WOMEN

Given what we have just said, it is logical that "glamour" photography embraces many styles of photography, and many styles of model. One market will demand the bimbo, the kind of girl where you shine a torch in her ear to make her eyes light up. Another market will demand the waif, to arouse protective instincts in men or to provide someone with whom very young girls can identify. Yet another will demand the kind of self-possessed young woman who radiates calm without arrogance. Then there are the ones who are, like Lord Byron, "mad, bad, and dangerous to know".

The older the subject, however, the more important it is that she should be portrayed with an inkling of her character; and in general, that character must be appropriate to her age. There are few very young models who can carry off an air of sophistication, or of haughtiness; but equally, as the subject grows older, it is increasingly hard for her

to look vulnerable or innocent.

The make-up must also reflect this. A very young model may appear either to be devoid of make-up (which is often the most difficult make-up of all to apply), or she may wear the most extreme colours and dramatic patterns, often called "fantasy" make-up. A model in her thirties or older, on the other hand, will normally be served best by conventional make-up, conventionally applied in the style of the time. It is important to remember that make-up dates a picture, and that if you want to re-create the look of a bygone period, you can often achieve more with make-up than you can with clothes.

"BEEFCAKE" AND MIXED DOUBLES

Although the overwhelming majority of glamour pictures are of women, there is also a significant market for glamour pictures of men, both among women and among homosexual men. For the most part, there are either moody shots with lots of chiaroscuro, or very hard-edge in an almost Socialist-Realist style; the style of lighting is much akin to the *notan* of classical Japanese art theory.

Mother-and-child shots can also have a certain aspect of glamour to them. As with any other glamour shots, this is because of the idealization which is expected in this sort of photography; at least for the moment when the picture is taken, all the less appetizing aspects of parenthood are forgotten, such as the sleepless nights and dirty nappies.

As for what might be termed "lover" shots, pictures of couples can be erotic or tender or passionate or of course pornographic; but "glamour" is probably the most appropriate category of photography for them.

THE GLAMOUR STUDIO

In general, you need a good deal of room in a glamour studio. The model must be far enough from the background that there are no problems with shadows, and there must normally be room to light the background

independently. You also need space to use lenses of longer-than-normal focal lengths; one of the great standards is 150mm on a Hasselblad, and some photographers like a 250mm lens on a 6x7 cm camera.

If you want to build room-sets, you need even more room. A "cove" or "jam-jar" is ideal, but it should be big enough to park two cars in it, side-by-side: a model may be a lot smaller than an automobile, but this is the kind of space you need.

It is of course quite possible to shoot glamour entirely on location, and a number of very successful photographers specialize in this. On the other hand, glamour photography by its very nature involves an element of fantasy and idealization, and the real world does not always lend itself very well to this sort of thing: lights are in the wrong places, radiators are obtrusive, electrical wall sockets come into shot . . . If at all possible, the built room-set is a much better idea.

Regardless of whether you are shooting in the studio or on location, you need facilities for the model and support crew; we shall come back to these after looking at the kind of lighting equipment you need for glamour.

LIGHTING EQUIPMENT FOR GLAMOUR

A rueful joke is that glamour studios need tungsten (continuous) lighting in the winter, to keep the model warm, and flash in the summer, to stop everyone getting too hot. In fact, the choice of electronic or continuous lighting for glamour is not really very important: it is more a matter of what the photographer prefers, which in turn comes back in most cases to what he or she learnt to use in the early years of his or her career.

Even so, although it is possible to create almost identical lighting effects with any type of lighting, there is no doubt that some types of lighting effects are easier to create with tungsten and others with flash.

LOGISTICS, PROPS AND BACKGROUNDS

As already hinted, the model's comfort must be paramount; it is extremely difficult to get a good picture of an uncomfortable model. This implies a comfortable, warm, private changing room, and a comfortable shooting environment. Sensible models bring a big, warm kimono or dressing gown to wear between shots, because a room which is comfortably warm for a lightly-clad model may be uncomfortably hot for the photographer and others; you have to strike a realistic balance.

You will also need a good, well-lit make-up area, whether the model applies her own make-up or if you have a professional make-up artist on the shoot. It is a very good idea to study make-up yourself and to keep a good basic make-up kit at hand. You need to understand what is known in the theatre as "corrective" make-up, so that you can fake out problems which often arise from late nights and over-enthusiastic boyfriends. The model should of course be reminded not to wear tight underwear if there is any likelihood of nude or semi-nude shots; marks from too-tight elastic can take hours to fade.

Props fall into two categories. The first is those which pertain directly to the model: principally clothes and jewellery, though things like hand-mirrors and hair-brushes can also fit into this group. The second is those which set the scene, which include furniture, drapes, rugs, and the like.

A very important point here is that most of the hire agencies specializing in props are geared to the television and movie market, where the camera does not linger on the props. When they are used for still photography, they may look very shabby indeed. Getting good props for glamour photography can be very difficult, very time-consuming and very expensive.

Finally, almost any backgrounds can be used, from the most natural to the most artificial. Unlike food photography, where so many backgrounds look contrived or inappropriate, the glamour picture is by its very nature contrived; there is a suspension of disbelief, a contract between the photographer and the person who is looking at the picture, which says (in effect) that anything goes. The only thing to watch out for is that the background is clean and neat; the least hint of grubbiness or shabbiness will drag the picture down faster than anything else.

THE TEAM

At its simplest, a glamour shoot needs only the photographer and the model(s). At its most complex, the photographer may work with two, three or more assistants, and there may be at least one each of make-up artist, hair stylist, props buyer, and specialists such as animal handlers, drivers, mechanics and (inevitably) clients, who always seem curiously enthusiastic about model shots.

The best team is usually the smallest which can handle the work to be done, though if the budget runs to it, an all-purpose make-up and hair stylist is an invaluable addition to the team.

THE GLAMOUR SHOOT

More than with any other type of photography, all the participants in a glamour shoot need to have a clear idea of their roles; and the photographer must be the ringmaster. He or she must have a clear idea of what pictures are wanted; of how the make-up should look; of how the model and the props should interact; and of when everything is supposed to happen. The besetting problem for the inexperienced glamour photographer is not being able to give directions, and the only way to learn how to do this is to work with someone who is experienced. This is usually another photographer, but it can also be a model; more than one model has opened her own studio, principally for amateurs and young professional photographers who get the chance to work with an experienced model for a very modest cost.

Until you have plenty of experience in working with models, you would do well to avoid "test shots" where both you and the model are working for your respective portfolios. The danger is that neither of you will really know what to do, which will damage the self-confidence of both parties, and make things worse rather than better. On the other hand, you may find it useful, if you can find an appropriate but inexperienced model, to try to re-create some of the pictures in this book, or from elsewhere: there are few better ways to learn. You may also find it useful to buy one of those little books or packs of cards which show scores of different poses, each economically sketched with a few lines, which show the model how to arrange her arms and legs. Using these rather tacky-looking posing aids provides an excellent starting point for taking glamour pictures; you can always suggest that she stretch her right leg a little more, or move her hand nearer her head or whatever, once you have the basic pose worked out. It is easy to attack conventional glamour photography for being overly slick, formula-ridden and conventionalized, or for that matter as being sexist and politically incorrect, but (as with almost any art) until you have mastered the conventional style, you will at best be very limited in what you can achieve in an unconventional style.

Having entered this caution, it is only fair to point out that a number of very successful glamour photographers are self-taught, and that conventional concerns about equipment are of minor importance: glamour photographers use everything from 35 mm to 8x10 inch cameras successfully. The one thing that almost all successful glamour photographers have in common is an understanding of the importance of lighting, whether that understanding is learnt or seemingly instinctive. If you have an instinctive understanding, the examples in this book may help you to analyze your work; and if you have to learn, you will be hard pressed to find a more useful source book.

the
glamour
portrait

► The glamour portrait should be idealized, but not impossible. As any beautiful woman can tell you, there are some men who are frightened by beauty, because "Someone as beautiful as that couldn't possibly be interested in me". The way in which you represent your subject may be a long way from her normal everyday appearance, but it must still be within the bounds of her believable self-image. In other words, you are very rarely trying to create the Jungle Queen or the Mistress of the Night. Rather, you are trying to create a representation of someone as they would like to be in an idealized form of real life.

Unlike those fields of glamour which require greater degrees of nudity, a glamour portrait can very easily be fully clothed, and glamour portraiture is therefore an excellent way for models and photographers to get to know one another. This can be particularly important if you chance to meet an attractive young woman who may be understandably nervous about modelling, and who would not consider even lingerie shots. Glamour portraits can be totally non-threatening and, who knows: if you are both lucky, she could even develop into the next "supermodel" — and you will be the photographer who discovered her.

Photographer: **Ringo Tang**

Client: **Personal work**

Model: **Fiona Sproat**

Make-up & hair: **Jasmine Moore**

Art director: **Ringo Wong**

Camera: **35 mm**

Lens: **85mm**

Exposure: **f/4**

Lighting: **Electronic flash, 2x300ws with honeycombs.**

Film: **Fuji HR400 processed as E6**

Props & set: **Background is a plain white wall**

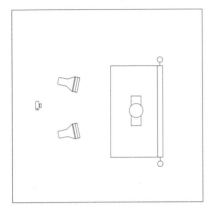

Plan View

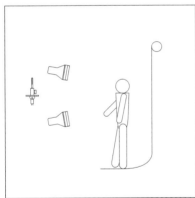

Side View

▼

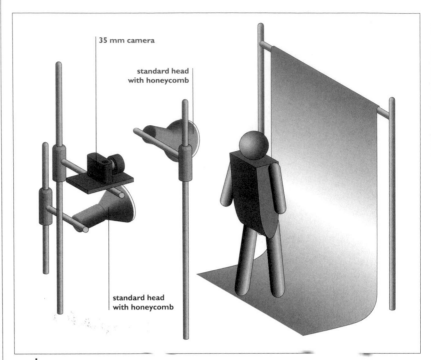

35 mm camera

standard head
with honeycomb

standard head
with honeycomb

IT IS RARE TO ENCOUNTER TIMELESS GLAMOUR, BUT THIS IS AN EXAMPLE. IT COULD HAVE BEEN SHOT AS LONG AGO AS THE 1960S, AND YET IT IS CURIOUSLY MODERN. IT ALSO ILLUSTRATES HOW GLAMOUR CAN BE ABOUT VULNERABILITY WITHOUT SUBMISSIVENESS.

Using shadows as part of a composition is nothing new, but it is rare to find them used so simply and unconventionally. As elsewhere in the book, the photographer has "broken the rules" to very good effect. The waif-like model is unconventionally placed and posed, and a huge, looming shadow dominates the picture. Both lights cast shadows on the background, which is normally something to be avoided. The model seems to be refusing to look at the camera, hiding behind those beautiful eyelashes, and we are left to guess why. To cap it all, the colour negative film was cross-processed in E6 reversal chemistry, which explains the strange and mysterious colours especially on the white background.

Photographer's comment:

The important thing was to achieve a delicate balance between the subject, the background and the viewer; the shadows were created to function as visual elements. The posture of the model was very important.

Photographer: **Salvio Parisi**

Client: *La Griffe* **(coiffure magazine)**

Use: **Editorial**

Model: **Angie Politte**

Make-up & hair: **Chen Ho**

Camera: **4x5 inch**

Lens: **210mm**

Exposure: **f/22**

Lighting: **Electronic flash: 3 heads. Soft box for main light, 2 heads bounced to illuminate background. Reflectors as shown.**

Film: **Polaroid Type 59 4x5 inch**

Props & Set: **White background**

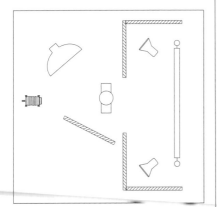

Plan View

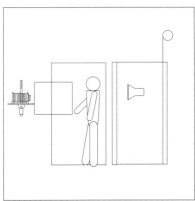

Side View

▼

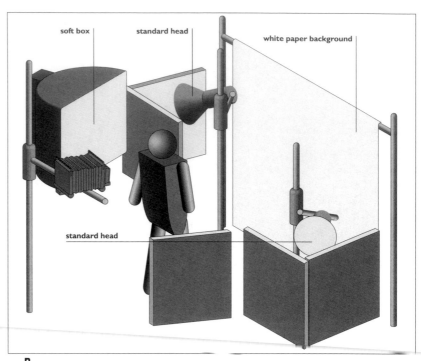

soft box   standard head   white paper background

standard head

Picture editors today are often more adventurous than they were in the past, and are less concerned with classically "correct" exposure and processing. Experimenting is always worth while — but only show the client your successes.

Often, the best ideas for experimental techniques come from trying to replicate accidental effects, or simply from saying "I wonder what would happen if..." Polaroid materials attract many photographers because they allow rapid experimentation; it can take less than an hour from conception of an initial idea to produce a finished, novel and highly effective picture. This overexposed and underdeveloped Polaroid has created distorted but recognizable colours, along with a superb high-key effect.

The lighting is simple but beautifully executed. The key light is a metre-square soft box just to the left of the photographer, supplemented by a reflector on his right (the model's left). The background is lit brightly and is absolutely uniform by bouncing the lights off reflectors, and the overall effect is classically high-key — which suits the exposure and processing technique perfectly.

Photographer's comment:

I was experimenting with Polaroids on a fashion/hair shoot; this is overexposed and underdeveloped, and I also tried an image transfer which proved very effective.

Photographer: **Robert Stedman**

Client: **Tobasco clothing**

Use: **Editorial**

Camera: **35 mm**

Lens: **135mm with 05M gel in front of lens**

Exposure: **f/16**

Lighting: **Electronic flash: single strip light with reflector on opposite side of model.**

Film: **Agfachrome ISO 1000**

Props & set: **Brown paper background**

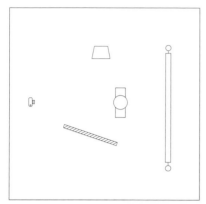

Plan View

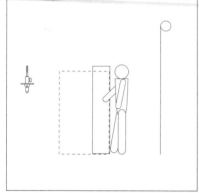

Side View

SUBTLE SEDUCTION

▼

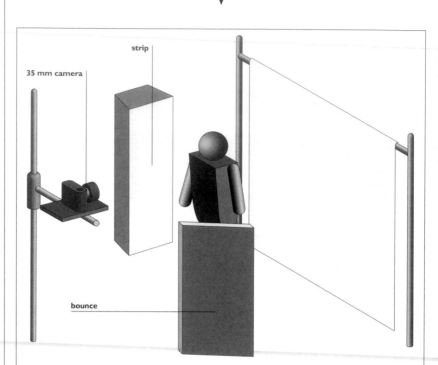

Sᴛʀᴏɴɢ ꜱɪᴅᴇ ʟɪɢʜᴛɪɴɢ ɪꜱ ᴀʟᴡᴀʏꜱ ᴍᴏᴏᴅʏ, ʙᴜᴛ ᴇxᴘᴏꜱᴜʀᴇ ɪꜱ ᴄʀɪᴛɪᴄᴀʟ ɪɴ ᴀ ꜱʜᴏᴛ ʟɪᴋᴇ ᴛʜɪꜱ ɪꜰ ʏᴏᴜ ᴀʀᴇ ɴᴏᴛ ᴛᴏ ʟᴏꜱᴇ ᴛᴏɴᴇ ᴀɴᴅ ᴛᴇxᴛᴜʀᴇ ɪɴ ᴛʜᴇ ᴍᴏᴅᴇʟ'ꜱ ꜰᴀᴄᴇ, ʟᴇᴛ ᴀʟᴏɴᴇ ɪɴ ᴛʜᴇ ᴡʜɪᴛᴇ ᴅʀᴇꜱꜱ. Uꜱᴇ ᴏꜰ ᴀ ʀᴇꜰʟᴇᴄᴛᴏʀ ɪꜱ ᴛʜᴇʀᴇꜰᴏʀᴇ ʜɪɢʜʟʏ ᴀᴅᴠɪꜱᴀʙʟᴇ.

Ultra-fast films such as Agfa's excellent ISO 1000 material have significantly more exposure latitude than slower films and are thus easier to use when you want both modelling and texture; you can capture chiaroscuro without burning out the highlights or blocking up the shadows. Also, although modern ISO 1000 materials are much less grainy than those of a few years ago, they still have a clear grain structure which can enhance many subjects; to some extent, the grain mimics or re-creates the texture and softness of the dress, and also unifies the texture of the fabric and the model's skin. As with any other "rule breaking" technique, pictures taken with fast films tend to be either very successful, or very unsuccessful; it is the photographer's vision that decides which it shall be.

Photographer's comment:

This was a shoot to illustrate a new line of clothing. The client wanted a lot of mood so we used the grain technique and side lighting.

Photographer: **Simon Chin**

Client: **Personal/promotional work**

Model: **Mimi**

Make-up & hair: **Andy Ho**

Camera: **6x7 cm**

Lens: **180mm**

Exposure: **f/16 for both exposures (double exposure)**

Lighting: **Electronic flash: single head in each of 2 double exposures.**

Film: **Kodak T-Max 100**

Props & set: **Model photographed against grey seamless paper; flower photographed on black velvet.**

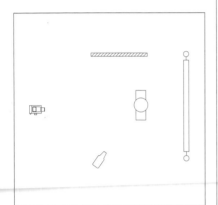

Plan View

Side View

M I M I

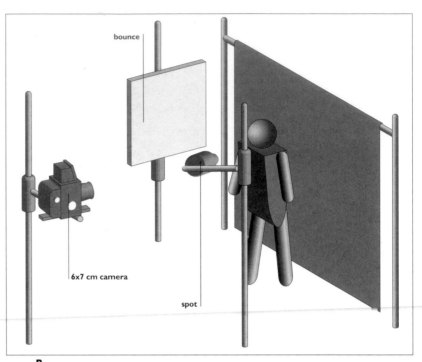

DOUBLE EXPOSURES ARE NOT ALWAYS OBVIOUS. AT FIRST SIGHT, ALL THAT YOU ARE AWARE OF WHEN YOU SEE THIS PICTURE IS THAT IT IS SOMEHOW DIFFERENT. ONLY WHEN YOU EXAMINE IT MORE CLOSELY DO YOU BEGIN TO UNDERSTAND HOW IT WAS DONE.

A 6x7 cm camera, as used in this shot, is the smallest format you would normally want to use for double exposures; larger formats such as 4x5 inch or even 8x10 inch are easier still because you can mark the ground glass more precisely and ensure better registration. The initial exposure was made with a fresnel spotlight on the photographer's right, supplemented by a small reflector beside the model's face on the other side. The second exposure, superimposed on the first, was made by shooting straight down on the flowers which were lying on black velvet; the flowers were lit obliquely with a powerful (3000ws) head on the photographer's right, with the angle being varied until the picture looked right. Black velvet is about five stops darker than an 18 per cent grey card.

THE LAST EMBRACE

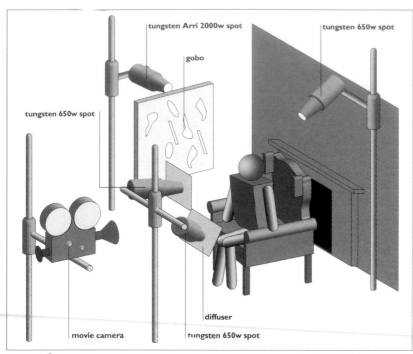

tungsten Arri 2000w spot

gobo

tungsten 650w spot

tungsten 650w spot

diffuser

movie camera

tungsten 650w spot

A PORTRAIT CAN BE FORMAL AND STILL GLAMOROUS. ONE OF THE FEATURES WHICH CONTRIBUTES TO THE FORMALITY OF THIS PICTURE IS THE WAY IN WHICH MOVIE LIGHTING IS USED, WITH FOUR SEPARATE TUNGSTEN LAMPS.

There are two 650w key lights from the front, one for the face and one for the legs, both softened with scrims. Another 650w spot back lights the hair and shoulder, while a 2000w spot shines through a gobo to create the hard background shadow.

Plan View

Photographer: **Ringo Tang** Client: **Bally** Use: **TV Commercial** Model: **Elisabath Eguazu**
Make-up & hair: **Caroline Nie and Maria Britron** Art director: **Caroline Nie** Director of photography:
Wong Wai To Producer: **Annie Ting** Director: **Ringo Tang** Camera: **Arriflex Ciné** Lens: **50mm
with #2 fog filter** Exposure: **f/5.6** Lighting: **Arri spot tungsten, 4 heads: 1 2000w through cookie,
2x650w front lights, 650w hairlight.** Film: **Movie film duplicated onto Kodak EPP 120**
Props & set: **Location at Regent Hong Kong, with clock, candle and flowers.**

Photographer's comment:

I wanted to create a provocative feeling, and to add atmosphere to the picture.

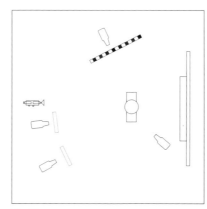

Photographer: **Ricky Loke Sai Ming**

Client/Use: **In-house calendar**

Model: **Carmen Creah**

Make-up & hair: **Selina Lau-Gomes**

Camera: **35 mm**

Lens: **70-210mm zoom at 150mm**

Exposure: **f/4**

Lighting:: **Tungsten main light 75cm from subject. Fill in from 35x80cm soft box.**

Film: **Kodak EES ISO 400**

Props & set: **None needed: very tight shot.**

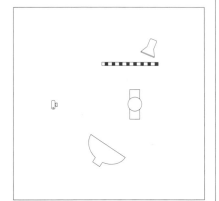

Plan View

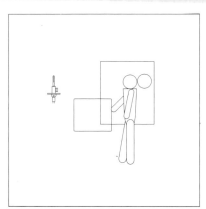

Side View

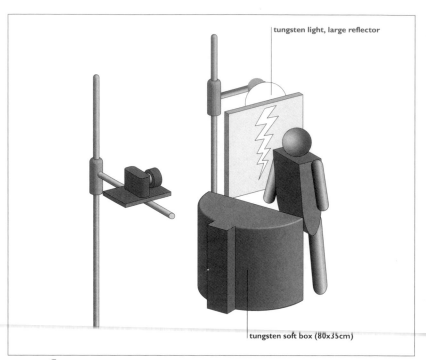

tungsten light, large reflector

tungsten soft box (80x35cm)

Excitement and vivacity are often hard to capture on film because they depend on the movement of the subject; a "bubbly" personality does not necessarily translate well to a still image. Ricky Loke Sai Ming used tungsten light with a daylight-balanced film, and a very lively model.

It is important in lighting not to be too hide-bound by convention. Our grandfathers would probably have found this shot unattractive; they would have complained that the lighting was unbalanced and incomprehensible. But to a generation raised on images from the paparazzi, the lighting conveys a clear message. It speaks of parties, night clubs and the "beautiful people" at play. By shining the key light through a cut-out shaped like a lightning flash, the photographer has created the sort of dramatic yet spontaneous-looking effect which we associate with loud music and excitement; and by using daylight-balance film with tungsten lighting, he has also captured the warmth and unpredictability of the lighting under which the paparazzi habitually work. The diffused fill ensures that the highlights are not burnt out and the shadows are not too dark.

Photographer's comment:

My aim was to create a "hyper" kind of shot, using the tungsten lights for a warm, exciting tone.

2 fantasy

Everyone has fantasies. They are often very personal, and some are more acceptable (and more believable) than others. Turning a fantasy image into a photograph therefore has a number of pitfalls.

The first is that a photograph of a fantasy is not necessarily the same thing as a fantasy photograph. The two can coincide, but a photograph of a fantasy may have a literalism which is out of place in the mood of the picture.

The second is purely technical. A badly executed fantasy always looks tawdry and cheap. What you are aiming for is a suspension of disbelief, a sort of dream-logic in which your particular vision is wholly believable. As soon as you see the wires which hold the flier in the air, the illusion is shattered. This is equally true of a badly done electronic image manipulation. Painters speak of "photo-realism" – but paradoxically, this is not always present in a photograph.

The third potential pitfall is more a matter of taste. On the one hand, a fantasy should by its very nature be eye-catching; on the other, it must inspire curiosity, interest, identification, rather than distaste. With fantasies, glamour photography is beginning to move away from the safe havens of portraiture, and sailing more upon uncharted waters.

Photographer: **Giancarlo Mecarelli**

Client: **Self-promotional poster**

Model: **Ana Laura Ribas**

Art directors: **Giancarlo Mecarelli and R.M. Delmotte**

Stylist: **Max**

Camera: **9x12 cm**

Lens: **210mm**

Exposure: **f/22 (main image)**

Lighting: Electronic flash: **3 heads. Key light, soft box 1.5m above model. Background lit by Evenlite with honeycomb, 1.5m from background, just behind model. Plinth lit by Evenlite with honeycomb, 2m from model.**

Film: **Kodak Plus-X Pan (main image)**

Props & set: **Props bought by professional prop buyer; background is painted cloth.**

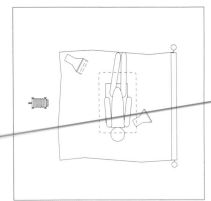

Plan View

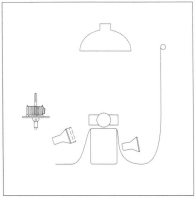

Side View

WOMEN IN TENSION

▼

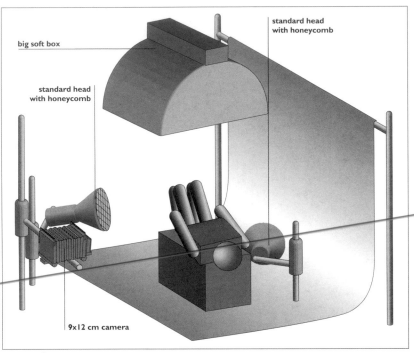

big soft box

standard head with honeycomb

standard head with honeycomb

9x12 cm camera

ONE OF THE MANY INTERESTING ASPECTS OF PRODUCING THIS BOOK WAS THE WAY IN WHICH A COMPARATIVELY SIMPLE TECHNIQUE — DOUBLE EXPOSURE — WAS USED IN SO MANY DIFFERENT AND CREATIVE WAYS BY VARIOUS PHOTOGRAPHERS. HERE, THE COLOURED "LIGHTNING" WAS ADDED TO A BLACK AND WHITE PRINT.

The original image is obviously a tribute to the Hollywood "Frankenstein" movies of the 1930s and even 1920s. Everything in it is consistent with that period: the wrinkled cloth background, the spike heels, the suspenders and gloves, and even the "electrodes" which look suspiciously like sink plungers.

The use of additional effects lights, as well as the main soft light, is also characteristic of the 1930s. Note the way in which the plinth is lit from the left, while the background is lit from the right, for a mysterious "doom-laden" effect.

After making a sepia-tone print from the original photograph, the print was copied onto Kodak Ektachrome EPP 100 Plus, and the "lightning flashes" were added by a simple double exposure through cut-outs in black paper; slight overexposure allowed them to flare.

Photographer's comment:

One of the pictures from a self-promotional campaign, it uses the image of traditional Italian motherhood, where feeding a baby means holding complete sway over him.

Photographer: **Mario di Benedetto by Wanted**

Client: **Imagic**

Use: **1994 calendar**

Model: **Louisa D.B.**

Image manipulation: **Alexander Koban**

Camera: **6x7 cm**

Lens: **180mm**

Exposure: **f/16 (Model)**

Lighting: **Model: Electronic flash;**

3000ws soft box. Leaves: Morning daylight.

Film: **Kodak VPL processed E6 push 2 (Model)**

Props & set: **Electronic composite shot using**

Paintbox

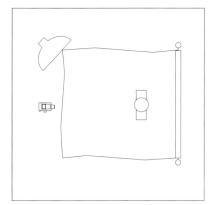

Plan View

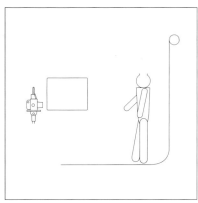

Side View

PRIMAVERA

▼

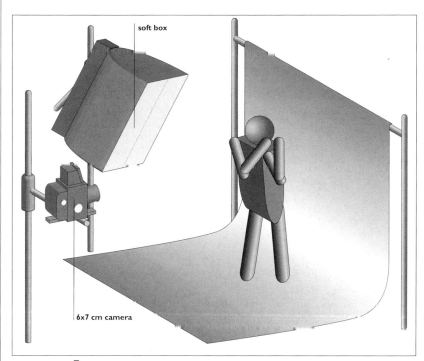

soft box

6x7 cm camera

THE FIRST ELECTRONIC COMPOSITE SHOT IN THIS BOOK, THIS IMAGE
ILLUSTRATES HOW ELECTRONIC IMAGE MANIPULATION CAN BE CREATIVELY MIXED WITH
TRADITIONAL PHOTOGRAPHY INSTEAD OF JUST BEING AN EXPENSIVE WAY OF RETOUCHING, OR
A TECHNICALLY INTERESTING BUT AESTHETICALLY IRRELEVANT TOUR DE FORCE.

Even more than a conventional double exposure, an electronic composite image exists principally in the photographer's mind. The process of creating that image is one of working towards something that no-one else can see.

The initial photograph of the model is simple enough. A 3000ws soft box, camera left, illuminated the model against a shadowed white background, with a large reflector board camera to the right to fill in the shadows. Likewise, the

photograph of the leaves started out simply: an ivy-covered wall lit by morning light. Then the fun started. . .

Leaves were selectively taken from the ivy-covered wall and combined with the picture of the model, with colours added electronically to the background; as the photographer says, it is extremely difficult to describe the actual electronic comping process, which was carried out using a Paintbox work station.

Photographer's comment:

This is a complex picture, with a great deal of electronic post-production.

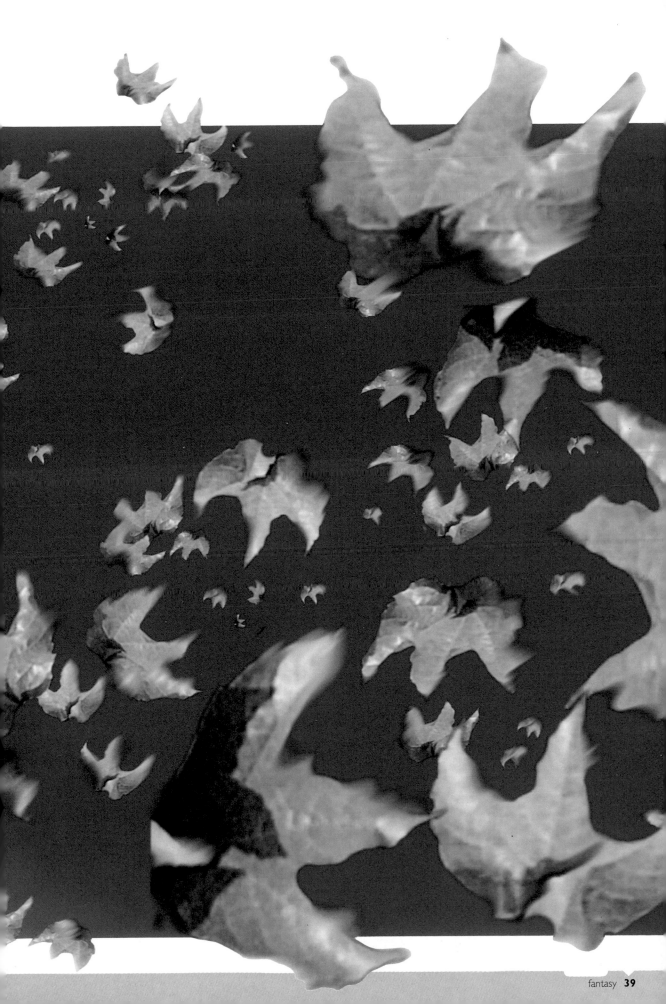

Photographer: **Marc Joye**

Client: **Self-promotional work/poster**

Model: **Edith**

Make-up & hair: **Marlène**

Camera: **4x5 inch**

Lens: **150mm, Sinar 80A filter**

Exposure: **f/16-1/2 (=f/19) x2 (double exposure)**

Lighting: **Electronic flash**

Film: **Kodak Ektachrome 100**

Props & set: **Sheets of paper; samurai sword. Greek portal was airbrushed on background.**

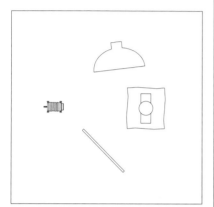

Plan View

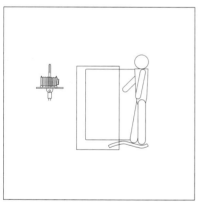

Side View

▼

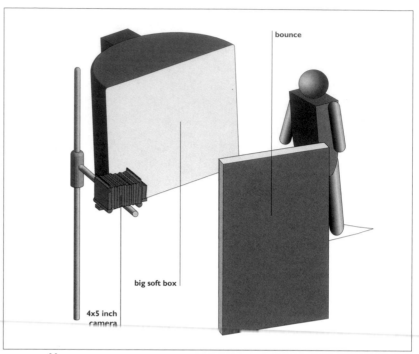

bounce

big soft box

4x5 inch camera

WITH THE RISE OF ELECTRONIC IMAGING TECHNIQUES, IT IS EASY TO IMAGINE THAT THE ONLY WAY TO GET PICTURES LIKE THIS IS WITH EXPENSIVE ELECTRONIC EQUIPMENT AND HOURS OF IMAGE MANIPULATION. BUT AS MARC JOYE SHOWS, YOU CAN ALSO DO IT THE TRADITIONAL WAY.

The first exposure contained everything except the two "floating" semi-transparent sheets. Although the model appears to be floating in the air on another sheet of fabric or paper, she is actually supported by a platform under that sheet. A soft light, camera left, provided the key light and a large reflector on the other side of the model provided some degree of fill. Several versions were shot before the second exposure was added.

The second exposure consisted of two sheets of paper, supported on lighting stands, which were made to look as if they were blowing in a soft breeze, against a backdrop of black velvet. They were lit from camera right, again with a soft box, but with a shadow board so that the front of each sheet was better lit than the back.

Photographer's comment:

I wanted to give the feeling that the samurai lady was floating on a sheet of paper in an imaginary space.

Photographer: **Jordi Morgadas**

Client: **Personal work**

Model: **Teresa**

Camera: **35 mm**

Lens: **105mm and 50mm macro (double exposure)**

Exposure: **f/11 (both exposures)**

Lighting: **Electronic flash: 1 head in each case, both soft boxes, 1 filtered blue.**

Film: **Kodak Ektachrome EPR 64**

Props & set: **Black fabric background**

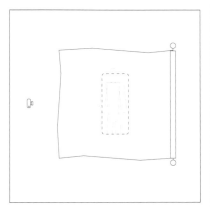

Plan View

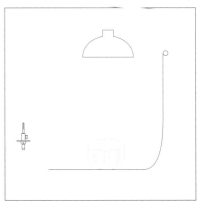

Side View

FLOR Y MUJER

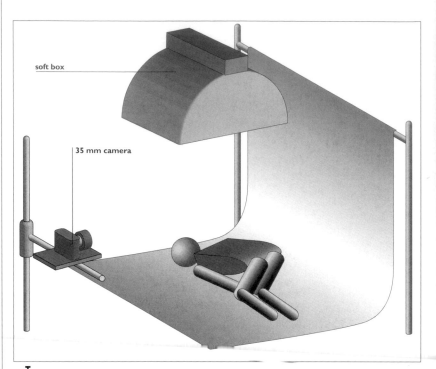

soft box

35 mm camera

THIS IS THE SORT OF PICTURE WHICH MANY PEOPLE WANT TO TAKE, BUT FEW MANAGE TO TAKE ANYTHING AS SUCCESSFULLY AS THIS. DOUBLE EXPOSURES IN CAMERA ARE AN AREA WHERE ALL TOO MANY PHOTOGRAPHERS FALL SHORT OF THEIR OWN VISION.

This is all the more true in 35 mm, where the screen is too small (and often too fragile) to mark effectively: with 4×5 inch or larger cameras, it is much easier to lay a piece of acetate across the screen and mark the relative positions of the various elements. However a gridded screen will make life easier.

The first exposure was made with a 100×100cm soft box directly above the model. The light was filtered blue, and the photographer used a 105mm lens. The girl was photographed against a black fabric background to make the second exposure stand out all the more: black velvet will not "read" if the subject on it is correctly exposed. The second exposure, of the flower, was made using a smaller 50×50cm soft box to light the flower as evenly as possible.

Photographer's comment:

The main thing about this picture, apart from the mood and aesthetics of the image itself, was the difficulty of execution. Making a double exposure on the same transparency, with two completely different light sources and lenses, was difficult.

Photographer: **Massimo Robecchi**

Assistants: **Bettina Muller, Teresa La Grotteria**

Client: **Dansilar-Collants**

Use: **Magazine advertising/billboards**

Model: **Giovanna Mazzi**

Art director: **Claudia Platania**

Agency: **G&R Associati, Milano**

Camera: **6x7 cm**

Lens: **110mm**

Exposure: **8 seconds at f/16**

Lighting: **Electronic flash & HMI; 60x120 soft box and 2 x HMI daylights to capture movement of fabric.**

Film: **Kodak Ektachrome EPP ISO 100**

Props & set: **Parachute harness; wind machine; coloured fabric (and tights); black fabric background.**

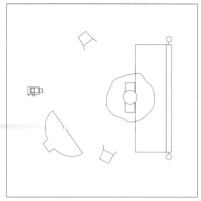

Plan View

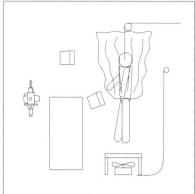

Side View

BUTTERFLY

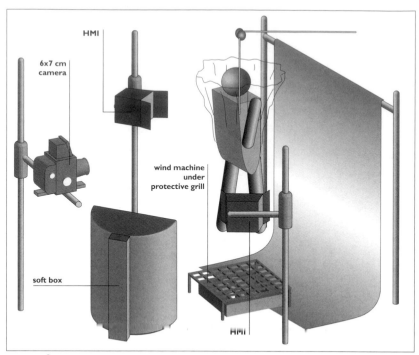

SUSPENDING THE MODEL FROM A PARACHUTE HARNESS, THEN USING A WIND MACHINE TO BLOW THE "SKIRT" UPWARDS, IS NOT SOMETHING THAT WOULD OCCUR TO MOST PHOTOGRAPHERS. HOWEVER, IT CREATES AN EFFECT WHICH WOULD PROBABLY BE IMPOSSIBLE TO ACHIEVE ANY OTHER WAY.

The soft box provided the basic exposure, but of course did not capture the flickering movement of the fabric; an additional 8 seconds or so of light from the HMI's added that. Using only HMI, on the other hand, would almost certainly have resulted in too much blur, in the legs as well as in the fabric. The studio had to be completely blacked out, of course.

The main difficulty with a shot like this is logistical. Once you have worked out the concept, it is a matter of experimenting to arrive at the details. What is likely to be more difficult is finding a parachute harness; securing the harness to the ceiling of the studio; and finding a leg model who is willing to be suspended in a harness.

Photographer's comment:

A butterfly is the stylized logo of the client so we wanted a butterfly effect. Using mixed electronic flash and HMI gave us the right balance of detail on the legs and movement in the "wings".

Photographer: **Giancarlo Mecarelli**

Client: *Strategia*

Use: **Magazine editorial**

Model: **Dusiene Ferreira Santos**

Make-up: **Agata Branchina**

Art directors: **Giancarlo Mecarelli and R.M. Delmotte**

Stylist: **Max**

Camera: **6x7 cm**

Lens: **180mm**

Exposure: **f/22**

Lighting: **Electronic flash: 4 heads. Soft box, 2 background lights, both with honeycomb grid, 1 with barn door, and hair/"hat" light.**

Film: **Kodak EPP Ektachrome ISO 100**

Props & set: **"Clothes" made of paper; paper background.**

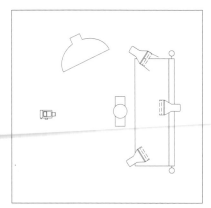

Plan View

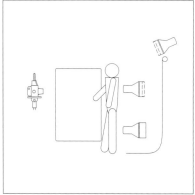

Side View

▼

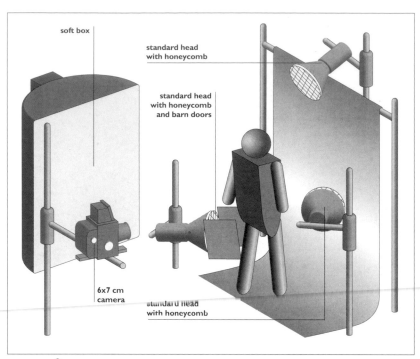

soft box

standard head with honeycomb

standard head with honeycomb and barn doors

6x7 cm camera

standard head with honeycomb

GIANCARLO MECARELLI IS MUCH SOUGHT AFTER FOR HIS ABILITY TO TURN NON-VISUAL CONCEPTS INTO VISUAL IMAGES. THIS IS THE ILLUSTRATION FOR A COVER STORY IN *STRATEGIA* MAGAZINE ABOUT THE USE OF PAPER AS A MEANS OF COMMUNICATION, PROMOTION AND MARKETING TECHNIQUES.

A large soft box is placed at 45 degrees to the model, camera left, to provide the key light. The 45 degree angle means that there is no real need for a reflector: the model is adequately lit, but on her left (camera right) her thigh fades away into the darkness of the background. This is supplemented by a light from above. The effect is almost that of a mediaeval clown emerging suddenly into the bright light of the stage.

However the background is separately lit, using two Evenlites, so that the model does not blend completely into the background; an important point is the significant distance (well over 3 metres) between the model and the background. It is this need for space which makes it difficult to take this kind of shot without access to a large studio.

Photographers: **Al Hamdan & Zivani**

Client: **De Millus Lingerie**

Use: **Magazine advertising**

Model: **Andrea Medeiros**

Make-up & hair: **Inês Costa**

Producer: **Hyran Matheus R. Guarind**

Art director: **Carlos A. Mota**

Camera: **6x7 cm**

Lens: **250mm**

Exposure: **f/32**

Lighting: **Electronic flash: 2 heads. Large soft box plus spotlight.**

Film: **Fuji RDP ISO 100**

Props & set: **Black velvet background**

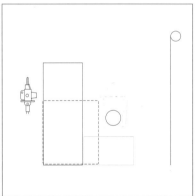

Plan View

Side View

▼

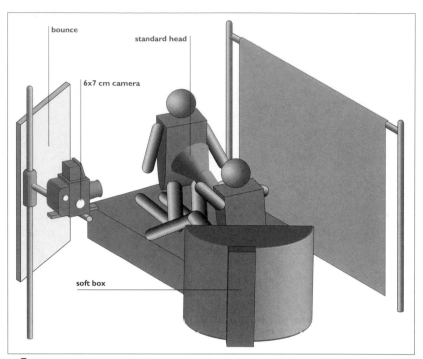

bounce

standard head

6x7 cm camera

soft box

THERE ARE MANY WAYS TO TREAT LINGERIE AND PLAYFULNESS CAN BE ONE OF THE MOST EFFECTIVE, AS AL HAMDAN ILLUSTRATES HERE. THE MODEL IS CLEARLY AWARE OF THE LIGHT, AND REVELLING IN THE POSE; SHE IS ATTRACTIVE, AND SHE KNOWS IT, BUT SHE IS ALSO STRONG.

The true key is not the 750ws spot, which is actually an effects light; it is a large, powerful (100x200cm, 3000ws) soft box to camera right, slightly in front of the subject, at maybe 60 degrees to the camera/subject axis. This provides an even, soft, overall light against which the contrasty effects light is dramatic without causing problems. This technique of using an effects light as an apparent key is an interesting one.

The image reproduced here is in fact part of a larger composition in which the man holding the spotlight is also seen. Instead of being an assistant, he is another model, and the couple are on a bed. This is reflected in the lighting diagram, though just the "apparent key" technique is shown here.

Photographer: **Günther Uttendorfer**

Client: **Sylvia Hahn Lingerie**

Use: **PR/Editorial**

Model: **Eva Baumann (Paris Elite agency)**

Make-up & hair: **Monika Wittig-Kuhr**

Camera: **35 mm**

Lens: **55mm**

Exposure: **f/5.6**

Lighting: **Electronic flash; 3 heads**

Film: **Polaroid Polapan ISO 125**

Props & set: **Shower built in studio from wooden panels, waterproof wallpaper, shower unit, hose and pool liner. Hot water provided!**

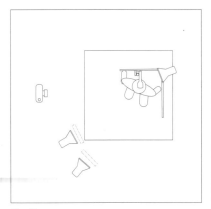

Plan View

Side View

E V A

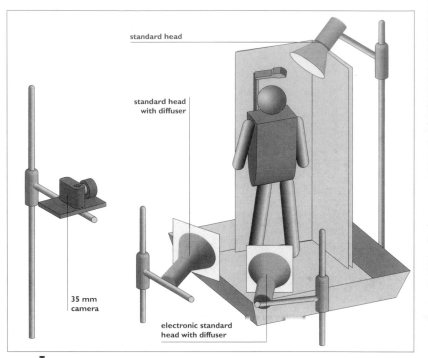

standard head

standard head with diffuser

35 mm camera

electronic standard head with diffuser

Τ HIS VERY DRAMATIC IMAGE SHOWS HOW WIDELY REGIONAL TASTES CAN DIFFER; SUCH AN IMAGE WOULD PROBABLY NOT FIND FAVOUR WITH ART DIRECTORS OR BUYERS IN SOME PARTS OF THE WORLD, BECAUSE IT WOULD MAKE THEM UNCOMFORTABLE. HOWEVER IN GERMANY AND SOME OTHER COUNTRIES, IT IS WELL APPRECIATED.

As so often, the difficulties in this shot were logistical: it included actually building a working shower, complete with hot water so that the model would not freeze, and spreading pool liner all over the floor in order to catch the water, which had to be removed with buckets afterwards.

The safety aspect was also important: electronic flash units do not mix well with water, so the two had to be kept well apart. The diffused directional lights from camera right were both about 5 metres from the subject, though the overhead/backlight was only about 80cm above the model's head, providing hair lighting and the dramatic overall contrast of the image. The shower was set so that the spray hardly bounced upwards at all.

Photographer's comment:

This was not easy to shoot but it was fun. We had to shoot fast, because even with hot water, the model got cold fast, and her make-up soon ran even though it was "waterproof." The shot also required careful direction (and a good model) to avoid being too sexist or even pornographic.

Photographer: **Colin Thomas**

Client: **Experimental/personal work**

Model: **Kate Charman (Matthews & Powell)**

Make-up & hair: **Paula Mann (Carol Hayes)**

Camera: **6x6 cm**

Lens: **180mm**

Film: **Kodak Ektachrome EPX 100**

Exposure: **1/125 at f/8**

Lighting: **Electronic flash: 4 heads. 2 soft boxes,
2 bounced standard reflector heads.**

Props & set: **Shop window mannequin painted
gold; painted canvas background.**

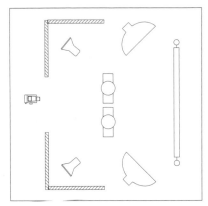

Plan View

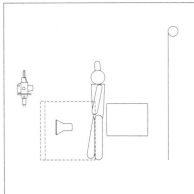

Side View

▼

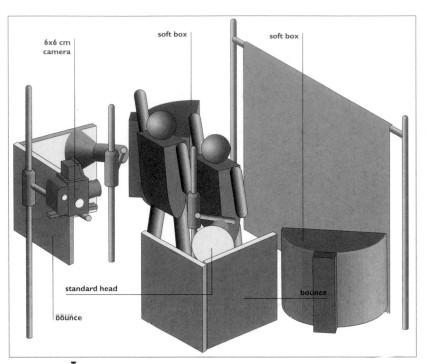

THE MODEL AND THE PAINTED SHOP WINDOW MANNEQUIN WERE
PHOTOGRAPHED IN AS NEARLY IDENTICAL POSES AS POSSIBLE, AFTER WHICH THE TWO IMAGES
WERE SCANNED INTO A 486/66 DX2 COMPUTER WITH 64 MB OF RAM, MANIPULATED
EXTENSIVELY IN "PHOTOSHOP", THEN OUTPUT TO 4x5INCH FILM.

Perhaps surprisingly, the two models –
live and mannequin – were shot
simultaneously, side-by-side, before being
comped together electronically, using
distortion, cloning, selective copying and
so forth. This image shows very clearly
that electronic image manipulation need
not be synonymous with inferior image
quality, as is often the case when low-
powered computers and cheap output
devices are used.

The main light comes from two
directions: look at the highlights on both
sides of the girl's body. Standard reflector
heads are bounced from two L-shaped
reflectors, each made of two 120x240cm
sheets, while the background is lit by two
soft boxes at 45 degrees to the
camera/subject axis, in the classic
copying/flat lighting set-up. Both are fitted
with blue gels to intensify the blue and its
contrast with the gold.

Photographer's comment:

*I shot this to show off my new digital manipulation facilities, so I wanted to make it a strong,
memorable image.*

Photographer: **Benny De Grove**

Client: **Personal work/exhibition/editorial**

Model: **Annick**

Styling: **Ann De Temmerman**

Camera: **8x10 inch**

Lens: **320mm**

Exposure: **f/22**

Lighting: **Electronic flash: 2 heads. 1 soft box, 1 background light.**

Film: **Polaroid colour image transfer**

Props & set: **Mask, rope and painted fabric background.**

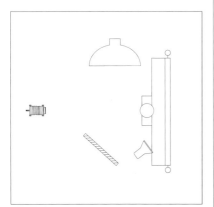

Plan View

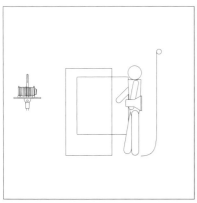

Side View

PRISONED JUSTICE

▼

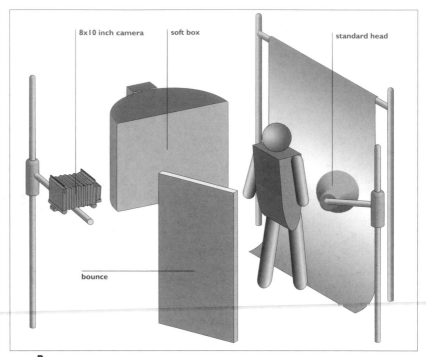

8x10 inch camera   soft box   standard head

bounce

BENNY DE GROVE'S WORK SHOWS HOW GLAMOUR CAN BE THOUGHT-PROVOKING. A BARE DESCRIPTION OF THIS PICTURE — A GIRL BOUND AND MASKED — SOUNDS LIKE A POOR FANTASY, BUT THE IMAGE IS REMINISCENT OF THE PAINTINGS OF THE GREAT SURREALIST ARTIST RENE MAGRITTE.

The light on the figure is classic "window light" or "north light", achieved with an 80x80cm soft box on camera left, about a metre from the subject; on the other side of the model there is a white reflector panel to provide fill in the shadows. The panel is angled so that the shadows are not completely filled; the lower left side of the model (camera right) is almost lost in shadow, adding to the mysterious, brooding quality of the picture. A separate light, just above the reflector panel, lights the background; as so often, a reasonable working distance is essential between the background and the model. Using Polaroid image transfer explains the rich yet strangely desaturated colours in both the model and the background.

Photographer's comment:

The mysterious nature of this picture is largely due to the lighting contrast and to the feeling of darkness which pervades the image. This picture was published in Focale, *a photo magazine.*

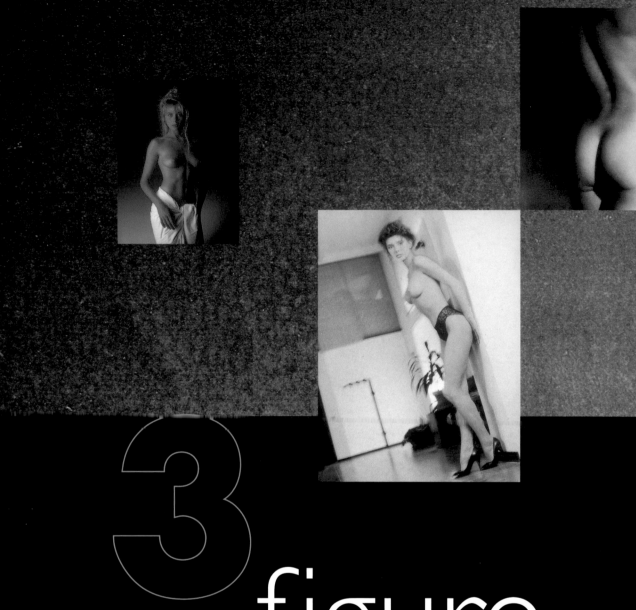

3

figure
studies

Figure studies, representations of the nude or partially clothed human body, have

been a staple of the fine arts for centuries. As early as the 1850s, photography was

inevitably co-opted to the same end.

Photographer: **Jordi Morgadas**

Client: **Personal work**

Model: **Nuria Galindo**

Make-up & hair: **Susana Muñoz**

Camera: **6x7 cm**

Lens: **150mm**

Exposure: **1/30 second at f/11**

Lighting: **Tungsten: 3 lights. 2 100x100cm soft boxes, 1 light illuminating background.**

Film: **Kodak Ektachrome EPR 64**

Props & set: **White background paper**

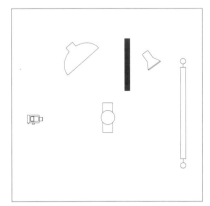

Plan View

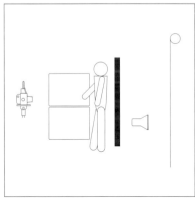

Side View

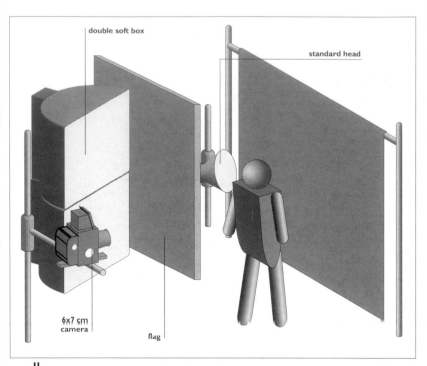

double soft box

standard head

6x7 cm camera

flag

USING TUNGSTEN ILLUMINATION WITH DAYLIGHT FILM IS OFTEN PARTICULARLY SUITABLE FOR NUDE AND SEMI-NUDE PHOTOGRAPHY. THIS IS BECAUSE THE WARM, REDDISH-YELLOW TONES ARE REMINISCENT OF FIRELIGHT WITH ITS SYMBOLISM OF HOME, COMFORT, RELAXATION AND SAFETY. THESE ARE ATAVISTIC MEMORIES WHICH MUST GO BACK TO CAVE-DWELLING DAYS.

Although it is fairly unusual to use tungsten-light soft boxes because of the heat build-up, it can be done: the modelling lights in an electronic flash head can be used in their own right. Here, Jordi Morgadas used two soft boxes, each 100cm square, to create what he calls a "column of light" 2 metres high and 1 metre wide. Placing them at 45 degrees to the model, to camera left, creates a natural-looking but contrasty light, reminiscent of late evening sunlight or firelight.

A large black panel protects the white background from spill light from the soft boxes, and allows it to be lit separately for a graded, warm background; once again, the effect is that of sunlight through the cave-mouth, or firelight. The overall effect is relaxed and intimate.

Photographer's comment:

This is a personal vision of Nuria Galindo, sweet, carefree and sensual.

Photographer: **Andrew Gordon Hobbs**

Client: **Mark Vasalo**

Use: **Test shot; proposal for advertising Lisa-Ho jeans**

Model: **Selena (Viviens Models, Sydney)**

Make-up: **Tania Travers from SPOTT**

Camera: **35 mm**

Lens: **105mm**

Exposure: **Probably 1/60 at f/5.6**

Lighting: **Tungsten: single 2K spot**

Film: **Kodak Tri-X ISO 400**

Props & set: **White wall**

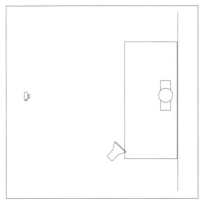

Plan View

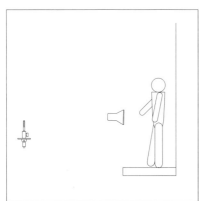

Side View

GLAMOUR IN FASHION

▼

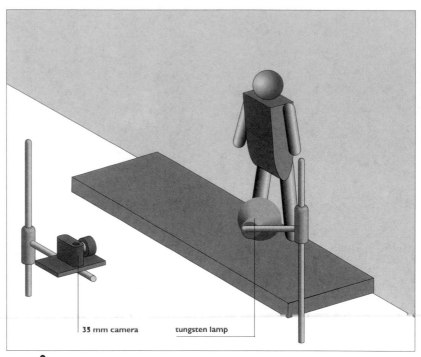

35 mm camera   tungsten lamp

ALTHOUGH HE HAD A FULL-SIZE STUDIO AT HIS COMMAND, ANDREW GORDON HOBBS CHOSE TO MAKE A FEATURE OF HIS MODEL'S SHADOW AGAINST THE PLAIN WHITE WALL. WHAT HE DID FROM CHOICE, A PHOTOGRAPHER WITH A SMALLER STUDIO MIGHT HAVE TO DO FROM NECESSITY.

The aim was to create the impression of bright sunlight. Obviously, the idea of an attractive girl wearing only a pair of jeans and leaning against a sunlit wall in the open has a certain inherent impact.

A single 2K tungsten spot a couple of metres from the model, provided the kind of highly directional light which was needed; an advantage of shooting in black and white is that the film can accommodate a wider tonal range than colour, without risk of the highlights burning in or the shadows blocking up. Baby oil on the girl's skin gave a sheen and added still more contrast, and a low camera angle accentuated the length of her legs as well as giving her a more dominant pose.

Photographer's comment:

Test shots for clients can allow the possibility of shooting your own way instead of copying a brief from an advertising agency.

Photographer: **Benny De Grove**

Client: **Personal work/exhibition**

Model: **Annick**

Camera: **8x10 inch**

Lens: **320mm**

Exposure: **not recorded**

Lighting: **Electronic flash: soft box overhead, background lit separately. Reflector between camera and model.**

Film: **Polaroid image transfer**

Props & set: **Painted fabric background**

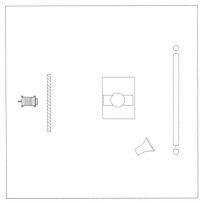

Plan View

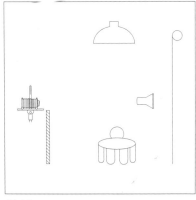

Side View

BACH TO THE BEGINNING

▼

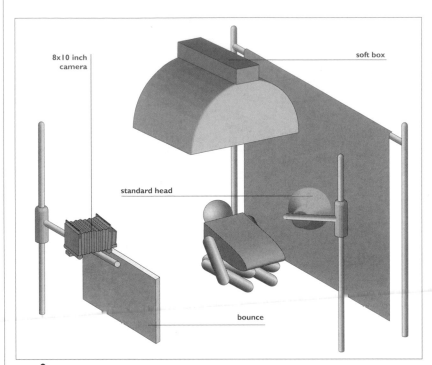

8x10 inch camera

soft box

standard head

bounce

Sometimes it seems that this book is more about breaking rules than about following them, but that is inevitable when you are dealing with leading creative photographers. A plain overhead soft box is something you would almost never use to light a nude — but it works.

The model's back hovers on the edge of overexposure; any more exposure, and it would have burnt out. The exposure, therefore, is the maximum which still leaves detail in this area. This in turn allows a curiously high-key effect for such a moodily lit picture, and it also emphasizes the vivid colours of the painted background. More importantly still, it allows the paper on which the image transfer print was made to play a significant part in the colour and texture of the image.

The main light is a 180x220cm soft box, about 2 metres above the model's back; the power of the unit is 6400ws. A reflector set at 45 degrees to the floor, so that it bounces light from the soft box onto the model's side, lightens the shadows as far as possible.

Photographer's comment:

The fragility of the model is accentuated by the overexposure of the back, so even the shadows are very light. This allows the colour of the paper on which the print was made to play an important part.

Photographer: **Judith Vizcarra Puig**

Client: **Portfolio work**

Model: **Judith Angrill**

Make-up: **Ruth Vizcarra**

Camera: **6x7 cm**

Lens: **180mm**

Exposure: **f/22**

Lighting: **Electronic flash: 5 heads, spot for key.**

Film: **Fuji**

Props & set: **White background and
posing blocks**

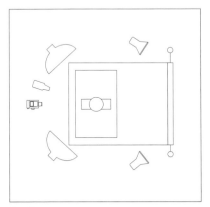

Plan View

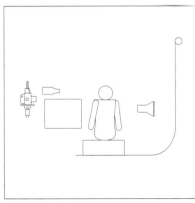

Side View

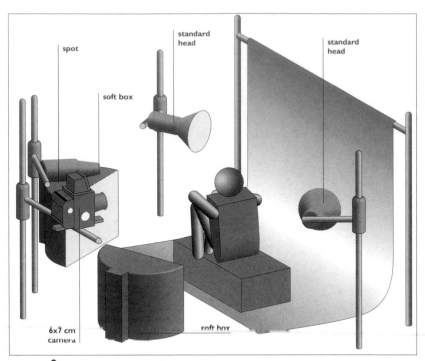

spot

standard
head

standard
head

soft box

6x7 cm
camera

soft box

Surprisingly, complex lighting characterizes this superbly-executed nude study which is both very traditional and very up-to-date. Use of no fewer than three lights on the subject, and two on the background, creates an excellent impression of roundness and shape.

Somehow, the ultra-modern hair style of the model in such a beautifully conceived and executed shot is almost shocking, but it shows how an understanding of lighting techniques can be applied to any subject.

The girl is lit with a spotlight just to the left of the camera to give an exposure of f/22, but the lateral fill-in lights on either side of the model at about 45 degrees are also set at a distance which gives f/22. The effect is in some ways similar to a huge curved light-bank, but it also introduces shadows and modelling which would otherwise be absent. Balancing the three lights precisely, so that there are no crossed shadows, is time-consuming but essential. The background is lit one stop brighter than the figure (measured with an incident-light meter) for a true high-key effect.

Photographer's comment:

The important thing about this picture is the simplicity of tones and shapes, contrasting with the detail in the flowers.

Photographer: **Jordi Morgadas**

Client: **TGD Tarragona Disseny**

Use: **Advertising poster**

Model: **Karin**

Make-up & hair: **Susana Muñoz**

Art director: **Jose Maria Rovira**

Camera: **35 mm**

Lens: **105mm with Softar II**

Exposure: **1/8 second at f/8**

Lighting: **Tungsten: 2 x 100x100cm soft box**

Film: **Kodak Ektachrome EPR 64**

Props & set: **Fabric; painted fabric background.**

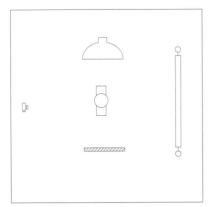

Plan View

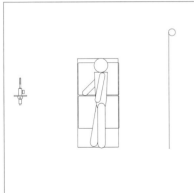

Side View

SUAVE

▼

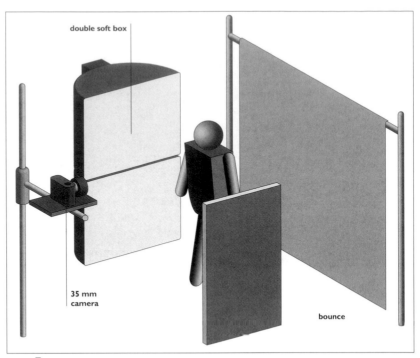

double soft box

35 mm camera

bounce

THIS CLASSICAL NUDE, WHERE THE CURVE OF THE GIRL'S BODY AND THE LIGHT ON HER BACK CONTINUES THE SMOOTH SWEEP OF THE FABRIC IN THE BACKGROUND, WAS ACTUALLY MADE AS AN ADVERTISEMENT FOR HOUSEHOLD FURNISHING FABRICS.

The modelling lights in an electronic flash head can be used as a light source in their own right. Two soft boxes, each one a metre square, were placed one on top of the other to provide a single large, soft light source measuring 2 metres high and 1 metre wide. This was camera left; to the camera right, again just out of shot, there was a large white reflector panel to fill the shadows.

Because modelling lights do not provide much light, exposures are necessarily long: in this case, because f/8 was needed to ensure adequate depth of field, a 1/8 second exposure was necessary. This places some constraints on the sort of pictures which can be shot using this kind of lighting, though exposures of 1/4 second and even 1/2 second can normally be attempted with impunity.

Photographer's comment:

The purpose of this shot was to convey an atmosphere of softness and gentleness in keeping with the nature of the fabric.

Photographer: **Gérard de St. Maxent**

Client: **Rossi Partners**

Use: **Press advertising**

Model: **Catherine**

Make-up & hair: **Stephanie Doratiotto**

Camera: **35 mm**

Lens: **210mm**

Exposure: **f/11**

Lighting: **Electronic flash: 2 heads. 1 soft box 150x150cm, 1 head to light background.**

Film: **Kodak Tri-X ISO 400**

Props & set: **Fabric wrap for model's hips, paper background.**

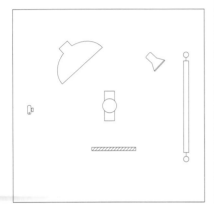

Plan View

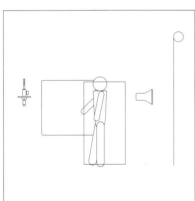

Side View

▼

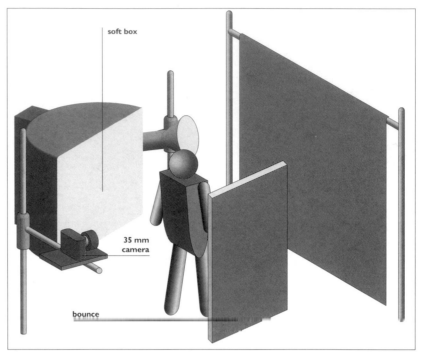

soft box

35 mm camera

bounce

Perhaps surprisingly, this is the only hand-coloured picture in the book. To some extent, the lighting is subordinate to the afterwork; but without the subtle gradation obtained through the skilled use of lighting, the afterwork would have been in vain.

The picture also illustrates the way in which photographs which at one time might have been regarded as unsuitable for general publication have now become accepted as part of mainstream advertising. This comes from a pharmaceutical campaign for a stomach medicine which, not so long ago, would have been rejected because of the very modest uncovering of part of the model's breast.

The lighting follows the familiar plan of a large light box at approximately 45 degrees to the model, camera left, but it is in this case supplemented by a reflector which fills in the shadows, unlike some of the earlier pictures in the book. The background is then lit separately with a small flash head.

The black and white print on partially coated paper was toned, and the fabric around the model's hips was then hand-coloured.

Photographer's comment:

Modest nudity conveys the feeling of well-being and the attractiveness of the stomach, which results from using this medicament.

Photographer: **Nigel Shuttleworth**

Client: **Personal work/editorial**

Model: **Lisa**

Camera: **6x4.5 cm**

Lens: **80mm**

Exposure: **f/11**

Lighting: **Electronic flash: single 500w/s head with 50x50cm soft box**

Film: **Fuji RDP 100**

Props & set: **Kitchen chair; black velvet background**

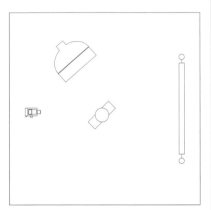

Plan View

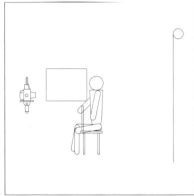

Side View

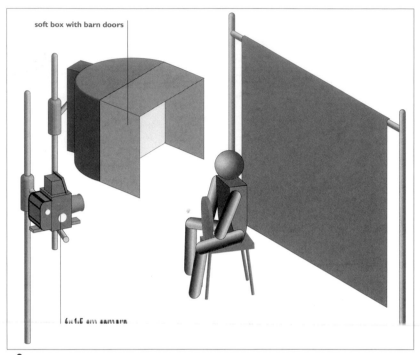

soft box with barn doors

6x4.5 cm camera

Considerable care in lighting is required if this sort of pose is not to degenerate into mere pornography; but the relaxed way in which the model is sitting, and the fact that you cannot "see too much", make this a useful exercise in lighting.

This is the sort of lighting which does not necessarily require a large studio, and which can therefore be duplicated even in a modestly sized room. Using black velvet for the background removes any problem with shadows, because they will simply disappear: the only lighting on the background is the spill from the key light, and so the background is too dark to register.

To make the light more directional, while still retaining its essential softness, Nigel Shuttleworth taped 50cm square pieces of black card to the top and sides of the soft box.

Despite the overall modesty of the shot, there is still an inevitable erotic charge as a result of the pose and as a result of the way in which the model is looking directly at the camera.

Photographer's comment:

An unusual nude study with the lighting creating an erotic, moody picture of a beautiful girl.

Photographer: **Massimo Robecchi**

Assistant: **Teresa La Grotteria**

Client: **Lingerie review**

Use: **Editorial & cover**

Model: **Madi Postiglioni**

Make-up & hair: **Gianluca Rolandi**

Art director: **Daniele Re**

Camera: **35 mm**

Lens: **50mm**

Exposure: **1/2 second at f/11**

Lighting: **Electronic flash (1 head) + sunlight**

Film: **Polaroid Polapan**

Props & set: **Reception area of studio**

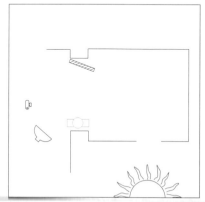

Plan View

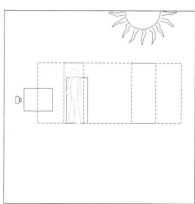

Side View

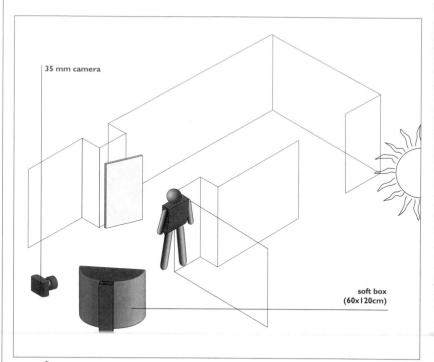

A⊤ ONCE DEFIANT AND VULNERABLE, THE MODEL LOOKS DOWN AT THE CAMERA. A HALF-SECOND HAND-HELD EXPOSURE ADDS A DEGREE OF BLUR, WHILE THE FLASH FREEZES ENOUGH MOVEMENT TO PROVIDE THE KIND OF SHARPNESS WHICH REVEALS THE TEXTURE IN THE UNDERWEAR AND THE FIRE IN THE MODEL'S EYES.

It takes a brave photographer to hand-hold the camera for an exposure of 1/2 a second; the risk of camera shake is too great. But what if you wanted a degree of camera shake . . . ?

How could you control the camera shake, and make sure that you did not lose too much detail? Answer: you could use electronic flash for its movement-freezing capability, and sunlight as fill. This is what Massimo Robecchi did here, with a single 60x120cm soft light to provide the flash exposure and sunlight as a fill in the rest of the room. The grain and unique tonality of Polapan instant processing film also adds a feeling reminiscent of old press pictures from the 1930s — something by Weegee the Famous, perhaps?

Photographer's comment:

I used the camera without a tripod for a demi-blurred effect during a long exposure: the flash light was to "block" the model and the sunshine was to fill the room with light.

Photographer: **Dale Durfee**

Client: **Self-promotional work for exhibition**

Camera: **35 mm**

Lens: **105mm**

Exposure: **f/5.6-1/2 (=f/6.8)**

Lighting: **Electronic flash: 2 heads. 1 spot, 1 diffused background light.**

Film: **Polapan ISO 125**

Props & set: **Background of dark, brown-sprayed canvas.**

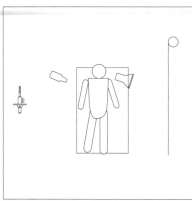

Plan View

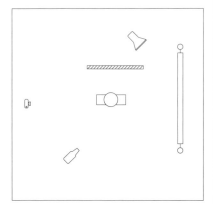

Side View

BOTTOMS UP

▼

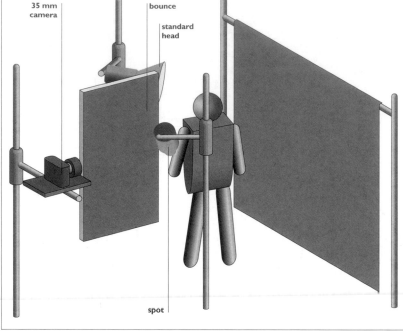

T HE TERM "FIGURE STUDIES" MAY SEEM SOMEWHAT OLD-FASHIONED NOWADAYS, BUT THERE IS STILL NO BETTER TERM TO DESCRIBE THE KIND OF DELICATE STUDY OF THE HUMAN FORM WHERE EROTICISM IS PRESENT, IF AT ALL, IN THE EYE OF THE BEHOLDER.

Dale Durfee is one of an increasing number of female photographers who are noted for their interpretation of the nude; she works with both sexes. Here, a deceptively simple lighting set up models the curves of the model's hip and buttocks against a subtly-lit background. A high-mounted electronic-flash spotlight, camera right and at approximately 45 degrees to the model, provides the strong, directional key light which creates the modelling. A polystyrene reflector board, camera left, bounces just enough of this light back to stop the dark side from being lost in shadow. A separately lit graded background shades from light to dark in the opposite direction from the lighting on the model, providing an extremely subtle but nevertheless noticeable contrast.

Photographer's comment:

The important things are the curves, the texture of the skin, and the simplicity of the whole shot.

Photographer: **Dale Durfee**

Client: **Self-promotional work for exhibition**

Camera: **35 mm**

Lens: **180mm**

Exposure: **1/125 second at f/11**

Lighting: **Electronic flash: 2 heads. 1 soft box, 1standard.**

Film: **Polapan**

Props & set: **Floor boards in studio**

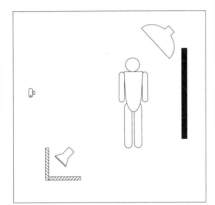

Plan View

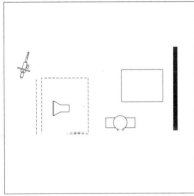

Side View

▼

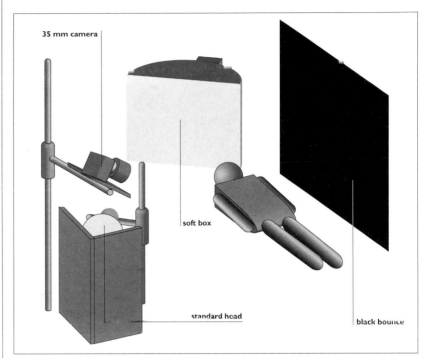

35 mm camera

soft box

standard head

black bounce

THIS IS VERY MUCH AN EXHIBITION SHOT RATHER THAN A PICTURE FOR REPRODUCTION; IT YIELDS ITS FULL IMPACT ONLY WHEN SEEN AS AN ORIGINAL PRINT. BUT THEN, MANY WHO READ THIS BOOK WILL BE SHOOTING FOR EXHIBITION RATHER THAN FOR REPRODUCTION.

Like much of Dale Durfee's work, this is a classic figure study; she describes herself as a photographer of people, and it is through her ability to relate to people that her individual style as a photographer is derived. The nudity is curiously asexual; this is a woman who happens to be nude, rather than a woman who has necessarily chosen to be nude.

The lighting set-up could probably be re-created with natural light in the right space, but Dale used a soft box behind the model to camera left to illuminate the model as if from a window: the reflection on the floor is a part of the textural charm of this picture. Then, another head was bounced from a reflector diagonally opposite the soft box, to fill the shadows slightly.

Photographer's comment:

The important thing about this shot is in the use of light on the skin to create a natural effect.

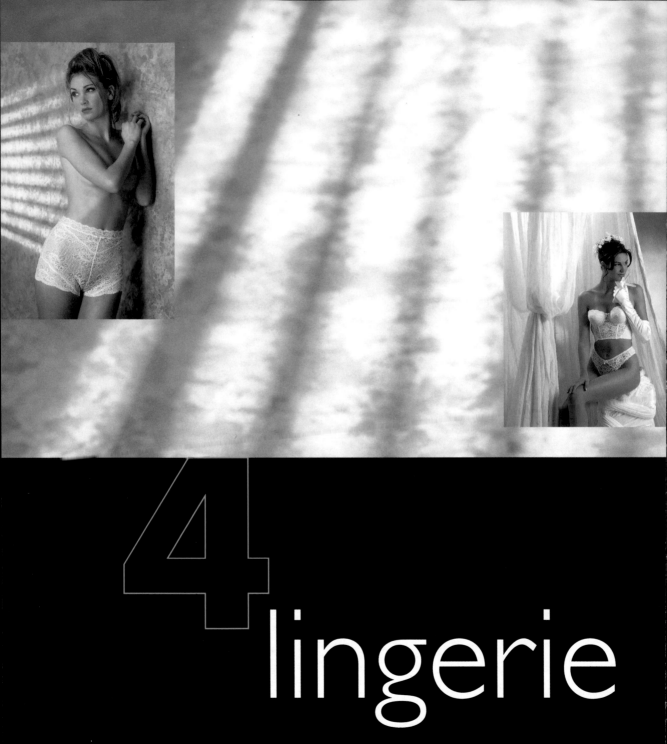

4

lingerie

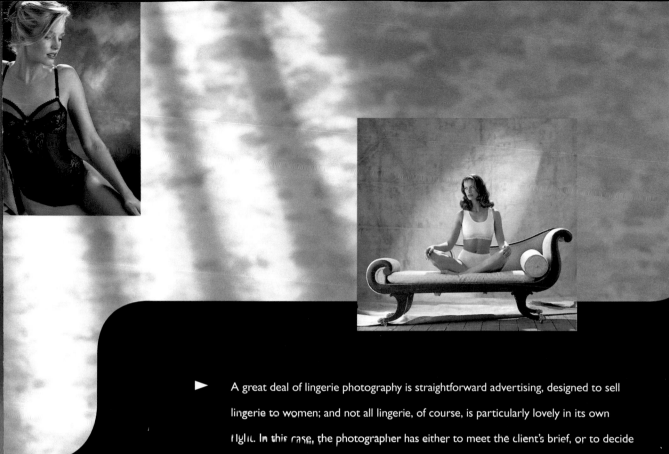

A great deal of lingerie photography is straightforward advertising, designed to sell lingerie to women; and not all lingerie, of course, is particularly lovely in its own right. In this case, the photographer has either to meet the client's brief, or to decide what sort of image the lingerie should have. Different aspects can be emphasized such as comfort, control, suitability for an active lifestyle, and so forth.

With prettier lingerie, fantasy settings may be more appropriate, but of course, if you are trying to sell to women, then they must be female fantasies rather than male. And, of course, one should not forget the type of lingerie pictures which are intended to appeal more to men, either to persuade them to buy a particular garment for their wives and girlfriends or simply because they like looking at pretty girls who are not over-encumbered with clothes.

Unless you are trying for a "just undressed" or "just dressing" look, make-up should be unobtrusive as it may distract attention from the lingerie. Even so, the lingerie should not overwhelm the model. As a leading French fashion designer is reputed to have said, "If someone wears one of my dresses, and people say, 'What a beautiful dress', then I have failed; but if they say, 'What a beautiful woman' then I have succeeded".

Photographer: **Michèle Francken**

Client: **Warner**

Use: **Advertising/brochure**

Model: **Helena**

Make-up & hair: **Rudy Cremers**

Stylist: **Sonja Mertens**

Camera: **6x6 cm**

Lens: **250mm**

Exposure: **f/11**

Lighting: **Electronic flash: 5 heads. 2 soft boxes, 2 spots for background, hair light.**

Film: **Kodak Ektachrome EPP ISO 100**

Props & set: **Painted background and mosquito net**

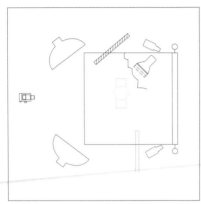

Plan View

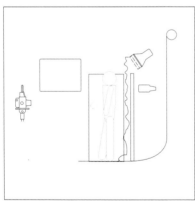

Side View

▼

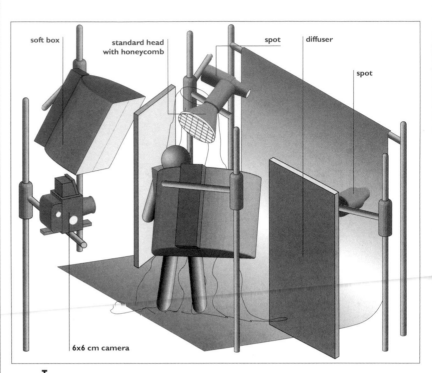

6x6 cm camera

THIS SHOT SHOULD BE CONTRASTED WITH THE PREVIOUS ONE, WHICH WAS SHOT BY THE SAME PHOTOGRAPHER WITH THE SAME MODEL AND THE SAME STYLIST FOR THE SAME CLIENT, BUT WHICH IS VERY DIFFERENT. ALSO, NOTE THE LATERAL THINKING: THE LACY WHITE FABRIC IN THE BACKGROUND IS ACTUALLY A MOSQUITO NET!

The underwear in this shot is altogether more frivolous than the previous set, which is reflected in the choice of accessories and props, as well as the pose: the model is altogether "softer" in her attitude, and more playful. The long white gloves and the flowers in the hair suggest a bridal connection.

The key light, as in the previous set, is a soft box, but this time it is camera right. In addition to the reflector, a second soft box set further away (two stops down from the key light) is used to provide further fill and good modelling in the lace. Two spots light the background, while an overhead hair light diffuses through the mosquito net and emphasizes the delicacy of the model's bone structure.

Photographer's comment:

This was one of a series of experiments made in the search for an appropriate style.

Photographer: **Jordi Morgadas**

Client: **Creaciones Teres S:A:**

Use: **Display advertising**

Model: **Eva**

Make-up & hair: **Barbara Urra**

Camera: **6x8 cm**

Lens: **180mm**

Exposure: **1/30 at f/11**

Lighting: **Mixed electronic flash (2 heads) and tungsten (1 light): electronic flash softbox and spot screened from model, tungsten soft box to light model.**

Film: **Kodak Panther PRP ISO 100**

Props & set: **Painted fabric background**

Plan View

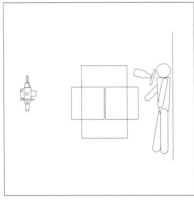

Side View

▼

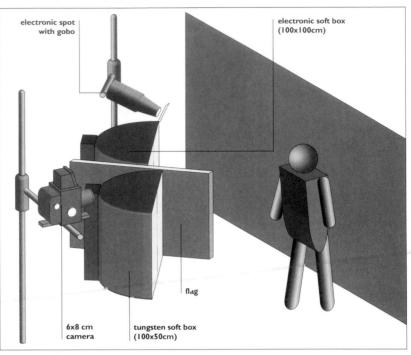

electronic spot with gobo

electronic soft box (100x100cm)

flag

6x8 cm camera

tungsten soft box (100x50cm)

FLASH AND TUNGSTEN LIGHTING CAN BE MIXED IN A NUMBER OF WAYS, AND ONE IS TO CREATE A CONTRAST BETWEEN WARM INTERIOR LIGHT AND THE BRIGHT, HARD LIGHT OF DAY. HERE, THE WARM TONE OF THE MODEL'S SKIN IS CONTRASTED WITH BRILLIANT "DAYLIGHT".

Jordi Morgadas employs one of his signature techniques here, using the modelling light in a 100x100cm soft box as a light source in its own right to light the model. By lighting the background with a conventional electronic flash 100x100cm soft box and a projection spotlight with a slatted gobo or cookie, he draws a very effective contrast between the two colours of light. A screen protects the model from spill from the background lights.

The choice of a blue-painted background with a mottled, time-worn appearance immediately conjures up images of the Mediterranean, which the bright "sunlight" seems to confirm; an excellent example of the creation of illusion through lighting. It is also an interesting thought that this picture would have been banned in most of the Spanish-speaking world when Franco was alive.

Photographer's comment:

By using two types of light in the same shot, the background can be a cool blue which contrasts with the natural warmth of the model's body.

Photographer: **Jordi Morgadas**

Client: **TGD Tarragona Disseny**

Use: **Catalogue/advertising/magazines**

Model: **Teresa Goode**

Make-up & hair: **Susana Muñoz**

Camera: **6x7 cm**

Lens: **150mm**

Exposure: **f/16**

Lighting: **Electronic flash: 3 heads, soft box, spot and snooted, plus reflector.**

Film: **Kodak Ektachrome EPR ISO 64**

Props & set: **Painted fabric background**

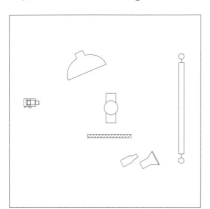

Plan View

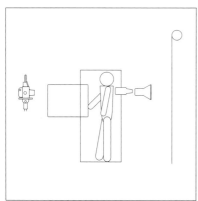

Side View

▼

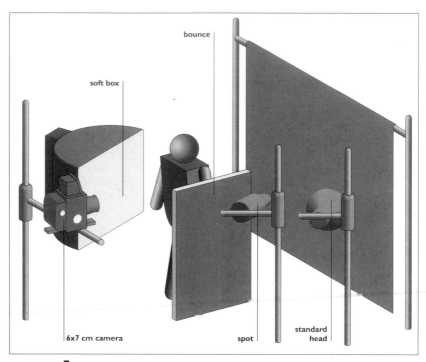

THERE ARE CATALOGUE SHOTS — AND THERE ARE CATALOGUE SHOTS. SOME ARE MERE ILLUSTRATIONS, TURNED OUT ON A PRODUCTION LINE WITH JUST A FEW SIMPLE LIGHTING SET-UPS. OTHERS, LIKE THIS ONE, ARE WORKS OF ART. THE DIFFERENCES ARE TALENT, TIME AND LIGHTING.

The key light is simple enough: a soft box 100×100cm illuminating the model from camera left, with a reflector just out of shot to bounce light back into the shadows. The exposure must be precise enough though to record detail in the model's black lingerie while still retaining a rich tone in her skin. Then, a powerful spotlight pours enough light into the "sky" of the painted backdrop to bring it up to the same kind of tonal value as the model's skin, and a snooted spot lights the rest of the background. Spill and reflections from the background lights create a surprising degree of back lighting, and the overall effect is reminiscent of stormlight, when the sun breaks through storm clouds.

Photographer's comment:

The main thing about this picture is its mellow lighting together with the harmony of the model's body.

Photographer: **Rayment Kirby**

Client: **Own picture library**

Use: **Calendar/editorial**

Model: **Tina**

Camera: **6x7 cm**

Lens: **180mm**

Film: **Kodak Ektachrome EPN 100**

Exposure: **f/8**

Lighting: **Electronic flash: 1 soft box + front projection.**

Props & set: **Flowers; background from stock.**

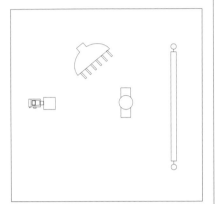

Plan View

Side View

G I R L   A T   W I N D O W

▼

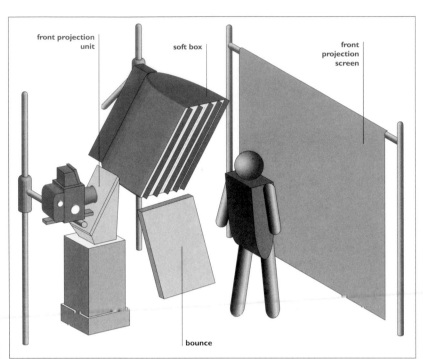

FRONT PROJECTION IS A TECHNIQUE WHICH FIGURES SURPRISINGLY RARELY IN THIS BOOK, ALTHOUGH AS SEEN HERE IT CAN BE EXTREMELY EFFECTIVE. THE SECRET LIES IN THE UNBELIEVABLY HIGH REFLECTIVITY AND DIRECTIONALITY OF THE FRONT PROJECTION SCREEN AND IN THE PURPOSE BUILT FP PROJECTOR, IN THIS CASE A BOWENS UNIT.

It is also important, when using front projection, to remember two other things. One is that lighting on the model or foreground should never be directly on the camera/subject axis, or it too will flash back from the screen, and the other is that the feeling of realism is greatly increased if you use some appropriate props as well as the model. There is always a temptation to use out-and-out fantasy backgrounds, but there is a risk that if you do, the model will not relate to her "surroundings".

The light on the model is a 750ws soft box with a slatted light restrictor on the front for extra directionality. Comparatively modest apertures (here f/8 on ISO 100 film) are necessary because of the power of the front projection system.

Photographer's comment:

This is simple use of front projection.

CHAISE LINGERIE

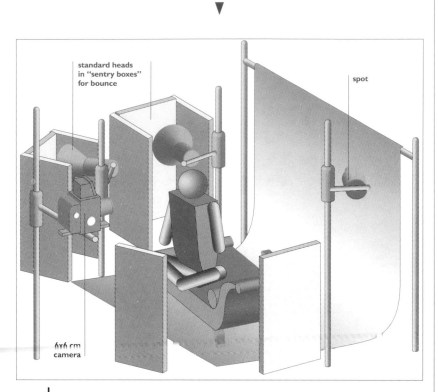

standard heads in "sentry boxes" for bounce

spot

6x6 cm camera

IF YOU HALF CLOSE YOUR EYES, AND LOOK AT THE AREAS OF LIGHT AND DARK IN THIS PICTURE — AN EXERCISE WHICH CAN USEFULLY BE CARRIED OUT FOR OTHER PICTURES IN THIS BOOK AS WELL — YOU WILL SEE HOW BEAUTIFULLY THEY ARE BALANCED.

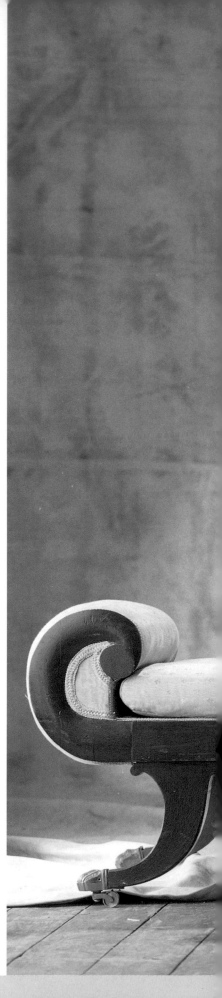

The effective key here is the background light, a powerful masked spot flash from camera right, which creates the bright, sunny ambiance and is reflected back with such intensity that it still casts shadows: look at the chaise longue beside the model. Fill comes from bounced standard heads in "sentry boxes" built of 120x240cm sheets of polystyrene, plus additional large reflectors to camera right.

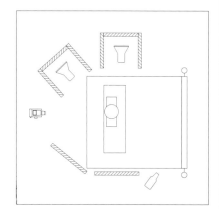

Plan View

Photographer: **Colin Thomas** Client: **C&A** Use: **In-store posters** Model: **Julie Townsend (Select Model Agency)** Make-up & hair: **Ellen Kramer (Artistic Licence)** Art director: **John Garbett** Camera: **6x6 cm** Lens: **180mm** Exposure: **1/125 second at f/11** Lighting: **Electronic flash: 3 heads. 2 bounced, 1 background light** Film: **Kodak Ektachrome EPX** Props & set: **Chaise longue; painted canvas background.**

Photographer's comment:

I wanted to emphasize the comfort and wearability of C&A lingerie.

Photographer: **Benny De Grove**

Client: **Knack-Weekend**

Use: **Editorial (Cover of *Focale* magazine)**

Model: **Mariet**

Stylist: **Bea Pecceu**

Camera: **6x6 cm**

Lens: **150mm with 81b filter**

Exposure: **f/8**

Lighting: **Electronic flash: 3 heads, spotlight for key, small soft light for fill, background light. Reflector also used.**

Film: **Polaroid colour image transfer**

Props & set: **Chair; painted cloth background**

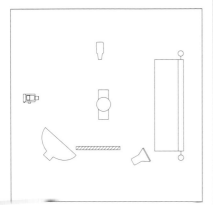

Plan View

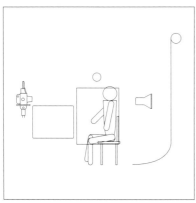

Side View

SOON MY SAILOR WILL COME

▼

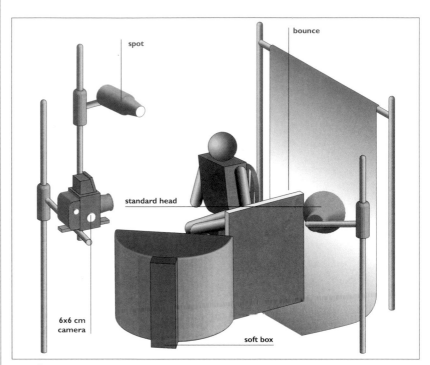

ALTHOUGH THE SPOTLIGHT TO CAMERA LEFT (THE MODEL'S RIGHT) CASTS A STRONG SHADOW ON THE FLOOR, THE BACKGROUND IS FAR ENOUGH BEHIND THE MODEL TO BE LIT SEPARATELY, ALLOWING IT TO BE GRADED FROM LIGHT TO DARK.

Because Polaroid materials lose a lot of detail, especially as image transfers, Benny De Grove opted to use a hard light to keep as much texture and detail as possible. This in turn implied a fairly strong fill from a low-mounted soft box, camera right, as well as a large reflector panel to bounce still more light back into the shadows.

What is interesting is the way in which this style of lighting suits the 1950s look; a look which is accentuated by the choice of chair; the model's formidably coiffed hair, and the orange-red colours which were so popular in those days. The colours are further enhanced by the use of the Polaroid image transfer process. The relatively poor resolution and the rather distant pose is again reminiscent of the 1950s.

Photographer: **Peter Barry**

Client: **Model test**

Model: **Maria**

Camera: **6x6 cm**

Lens: **150mm with Kodak Wratten 81C warming filter**

Exposure: **f/11**

Lighting: **Electronic flash: single soft box.**

Film: **Kodak Ektachrome 64**

Props & set: **Hand-painted backdrop**

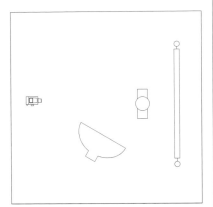

Plan View

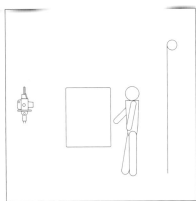

Side View

GIRL IN TEDDY

▼

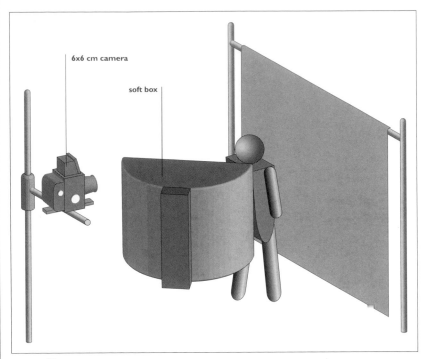

6x6 cm camera

soft box

Wɪᴛʜ ᴛʜᴇ ʀɪɢʜᴛ ᴍᴏᴅᴇʟ, ᴛʜᴇ ʀɪɢʜᴛ ᴄʟᴏᴛʜᴇꜱ, ᴛʜᴇ ʀɪɢʜᴛ ᴘᴏꜱᴇ ᴀɴᴅ ᴛʜᴇ ʀɪɢʜᴛ ʙᴀᴄᴋɢʀᴏᴜɴᴅ — ᴀɴᴅ ᴏꜰ ᴄᴏᴜʀꜱᴇ ᴛʜᴇ ʀɪɢʜᴛ ᴘʜᴏᴛᴏɢʀᴀᴘʜᴇʀ — ᴇᴠᴇɴ ᴛʜᴇ ꜱɪᴍᴘʟᴇꜱᴛ ʟɪɢʜᴛɪɴɢ ᴄᴀɴ ᴄʀᴇᴀᴛᴇ ᴀ ɢʀᴇᴀᴛ ᴘɪᴄᴛᴜʀᴇ. Tʜɪꜱ ɪꜱ ʟɪᴛ ᴡɪᴛʜ ᴀ ꜱɪɴɢʟᴇ ꜱᴏꜰᴛ ʙᴏx ᴛᴏ ᴄᴀᴍᴇʀᴀ ʀɪɢʜᴛ.

This is one of the comparatively few shots in this book which could relatively be easily duplicated without a large studio set-up: the model is not even very far from the background, and there is only one light. On the other hand, it is not always easy to find models this attractive or skilled at posing, or clothes which are so appropriate. Faced with such devastating simplicity, one cannot but admit that in the final analysis, what makes any picture successful is the photographer's eye alone.

As noted elsewhere, a glamour photographer need not (and indeed should not) conform to the popular image of a Casanova, but he may well have a certain spark which always seems to bring out the best in models. Female glamour photographers are often less dramatic, but in some ways more sympathetic.

Photographer's comment:

I wanted the picture to be warm and soft.

5
traditional
glamour

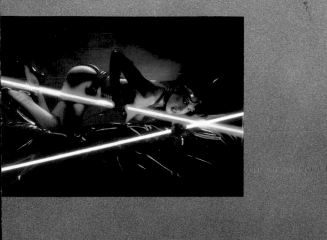

► Perhaps sadly, traditional glamour is somewhat in decline. These are the pictures which used to adorn calendars in every garage, and which were a staple of men's magazines: pretty young girls, very scantily clad (though rarely entirely nude), and usually smiling pertly at the camera.

This sort of photography has been caught in a pincer movement from two widely different directions. On the one flank, there is the question of Political Correctness: it is now far less socially acceptable than it was for a man to admit to admiring pictures of pretty girls. On the other flank, the old-fashioned men's magazines have had to "go pink" (in the jargon of the trade) in order to compete with ever more explicit videos. As a former editor put it, "Videos have all the same stuff as the magazines, and it jiggles".

To modern eyes, there is a sort of innocence to traditional glamour pictures which is rather charming; and indeed, because of changing public mood, many more girls may be willing to pose for such pictures than once was the case. The models must however be young and very pretty indeed if the picture is to be successful; very few girls are ideal models for this sort of photography.

Photographer: **Peter Barry**

Client: **Model test**

Model: **Tracy**

Make-up & hair: **Gillian Shepherd**

Camera: **6x6 cm**

Lens: **80mm**

Exposure: **f/11**

Lighting: **Electronic flash: ring flash on camera.**

Film: **Kodak Ektachrome 64**

Props & set: **Tall cuboid stand; gold painted
telephone. Background is blue Colorama
seamless paper sprayed with gold paint.**

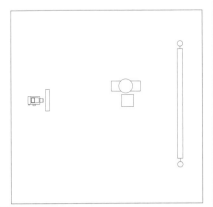

Plan View

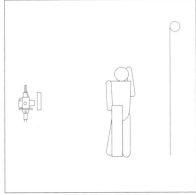

Side View

HOMAGE TO VARGAS

▼

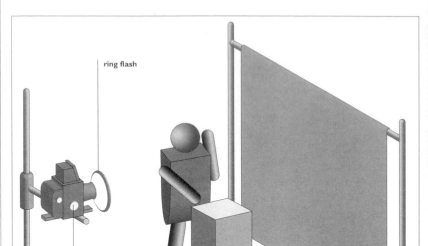

THE FLAT LIGHTING OF A RING FLASH MIGHT SEEM TO BE THE EXACT OPPOSITE OF WHAT
YOU WOULD NEED TO SHOW THE ROUNDNESS AND MODELLING OF A PRETTY GIRL, BUT IN
FACT IT CREATES HIGHLIGHTS AND SHADOWS WHICH ARE (OR CAN BE) VERY EFFECTIVE INDEED.

If you look very hard at the background,
you can just see the suggestion of a
shadow surrounding the girl's body,
but you would only dream of looking
for it after someone had told you that
this photograph was shot with a ring
flash. Certainly, this is the very opposite
of the harsh, dead pictures which
periodically appear as publicity material
for rock bands, usually when an
inexperienced photographer imagines
that he is the first to discover ring flash

portraits. Admittedly, this is a bigger
and more powerful ring flash than
most, powered by a separate
Quadmatic flash generator, but it
shows how even the most unlikely
techniques, used properly, can produce
very successful results. Successful
photographers are constantly asking
"What would happen if . . . ?" and then
trying it to find out. Unsuccessful
photographers may wonder, but they
don't try to find out.

Photographer's comment:

*I wanted to contrast the angular pose and props with her beautifully curvaceous body and
good legs.*

Photographer: **Peter Barry**

Client: **Model test**

Model: **Jackie**

Camera: **6x6 cm**

Lens: **110mm**

Exposure: **f/8**

Lighting: **Electronic flash: I head, bounced into L-shaped reflector.**

Film: **Kodak Ektachrome 64**

Props & set: **Tarpaulin/canvas sheet**

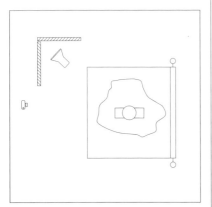

Plan View

Side View

▼

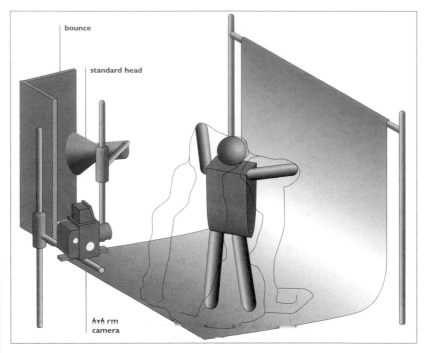

THERE IS AN ALMOST CHILD-LIKE SENSE OF PLAYFULNESS IN THIS PICTURE, THOUGH THE AGE AND STATE OF UNDRESS OF THE MODEL MAKE IT CLEAR THAT THIS IS PLAYTIME FOR GROWN-UPS. THE CONTRASTS OF LIGHT, SHADE AND TEXTURE ARE CURIOUSLY PAINTERLY.

Unless a photographer is working to an art director's clear brief, it is always a good idea to allow unplanned pictures some place in a shoot. In fact, even if he or she is working to a tight brief, it is generally a good idea to shoot extra pictures outside the brief if they suggest them themselves, and if there is time. Surprisingly often, when faced with a choice between the original concept and the photographer's improvisation, the client will choose the improvisation. Needless to say, the original brief must be shot too!

The "Rembrandt" lighting here is created by bouncing a single head into an L-shaped reflector to camera left; the reflector is made of two large flats, each 120x240cm. The background is lit only by spill from this.

Photographer's comment:

The attraction of this picture lies in the contrast between the softness of the girl's body and the harshness and roughness of the canvas.

Photographer: **Peter Barry**

Client: **Model test**

Model: **Fia**

Camera: **6x6 cm**

Lens: **250mm with Kodak Wratten 81C warming filter**

Exposure: **f/16**

Lighting: **Electronic flash: 2 heads. 1 large dish reflector with diffuser, one focusing spot with gobo.**

Film: **Kodak Ektachrome 64**

Props & set: **White Colorama seamless paper. The real prop is the girl's playfulness.**

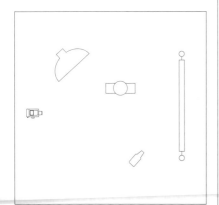

Plan View

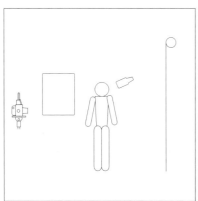

Side View

CHEEKY GIRL

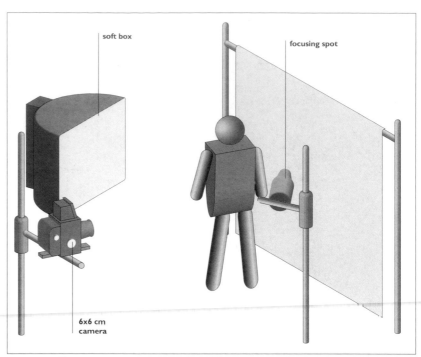

Even an experienced glamour photographer finds some models more sympathetic than others, and the interplay between the model and the photographer can often be allowed with advantage to influence the course of the shoot, rather than sticking to a preconceived shot plan.

The key light is quite strongly to camera left, with no fill, as you can see from the shadows on the model's back. A large reflector, even with a diffuser on it, gives a different quality of light to a soft box. The effect is somewhat akin to early morning light, an impression reinforced by the pools of "sunlight" thrown on the background by the focusing spot. These in turn concentrate attention to the expression on the girl's face, which is really a delightfully playful smile. The background is also lit by spill from the key light, and is uniformly lighter than the girl's skin tone for good differentiation. However, very precise exposure stops the white bikini bottom from burning out to a featureless white.

Photographer's comment:

I wanted to capture her cheekiness whilst not allowing anything to be seen but a promise!

NEON AND KODAK

▼

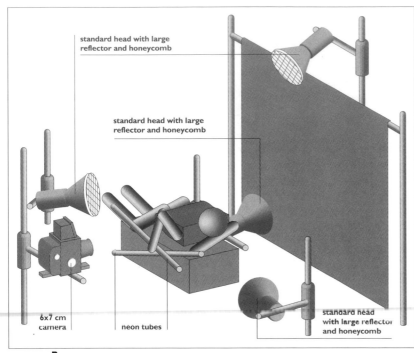

standard head with large
reflector and honeycomb

standard head with large
reflector and honeycomb

6x7 cm
camera

neon tubes

standard head
with large reflector
and honeycomb

Photographer: **Giancarlo Mecarelli**

Client: **Kodak**

Use: **Advertising/1994 Catalogue**

Model: **Patrizia Marcacci**

Make-up & hair: **Debora Sasso**

Art directors: **Giancarlo Mecarelli and
R.M. Delmotte**

Stylist: **Max**

Camera: **6x7 cm**

Lens: **180mm**

Exposure: **1/2 second at f/11**

Lighting: **Electronic flash (4 heads), neon tubes**

Bᴇɪɴɢ ᴀsᴋᴇᴅ ʙʏ Kᴏᴅᴀᴋ ᴛᴏ ᴛᴀᴋᴇ ᴀ sʜᴏᴛ ᴛᴏ ᴀᴅᴠᴇʀᴛɪsᴇ ꜰɪʟᴍ ɪs ʀᴀᴛʜᴇʀ ʟɪᴋᴇ ʙᴇɪɴɢ ᴀsᴋᴇᴅ ʙʏ ᴛʜᴇ Pᴏᴘᴇ ᴛᴏ ᴘʀᴇᴀᴄʜ ᴀ ʜᴏᴍɪʟʏ. Eɪᴛʜᴇʀ ʏᴏᴜ ɢᴏ ꜰᴏʀ ᴛʜᴇ sᴀꜰᴇ ᴀɴᴅ ᴛʜᴇ ᴘʀᴇᴅɪᴄᴛᴀʙʟᴇ — ᴏʀ ʏᴏᴜ ᴘᴜʟʟ ᴏᴜᴛ ᴀʟʟ ᴛʜᴇ sᴛᴏᴘs ᴀɴᴅ ᴘʀᴏᴅᴜᴄᴇ sᴏᴍᴇᴛʜɪɴɢ ᴛʜᴀᴛ ᴘᴇᴏᴘʟᴇ ᴀʀᴇ ʀᴇᴀʟʟʏ ɢᴏɪɴɢ ᴛᴏ ʀᴇᴍᴇᴍʙᴇʀ.

Any shot that mixes continuous lighting and flash requires a modest degree of mental gymnastics. Across the normal shutter speed range, the flash exposure is affected only by aperture, but the exposure from the continuous source is affected by both aperture and shutter speed. Of course, the two effects have to be added together. No matter how carefully you meter, Polaroid tests are normally the only way to get the final exposure right.

Although the main light might seem to come from the neon tubes, the electronic flash is essential to establish modelling, to show the background and so forth. One honeycombed Evenlite to camera left lights her legs; another to camera right, lights her face; another lights her back from above; and a fourth, again with honeycomb, lights the background.

Photographer's comment:

This is a commercial picture for the 1994 Kodak catalogue to symbolize the new Panther film which has better colours and better quality than traditional films.

Film: **Kodak Ektachrome Panther 100 PRP**
Props & set: **Neon tubes, vinyl covered sofa, paper background, plastic tubing (for model's costume).**

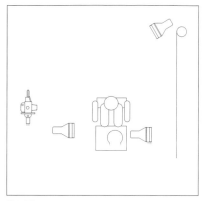

Side View

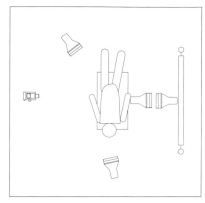

Plan View

Photographer: **Giancarlo Mecarelli**

Client: **L'Europeo**

Use: **Magazine editorial — cover story**

Model: **Ana Laura Ribas**

Make-up: **Carmen Amaro**

Art directors: **Giancarlo Mecarelli and**
R.M. Delmotte

Stylist: **Max**

Camera: **6x7 cm**

Lens: **180mm**

Exposure: **f/22**

Lighting: **Electronic flash: 4 heads. Soft box &**
Evenlite to light model, 2 heads to light
background.

Film: **Kodak Ektachrome EPP 100 Plus**

Props & set: **Model car; paper background**

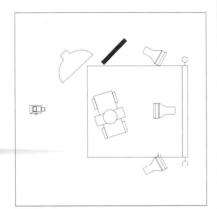

Plan View

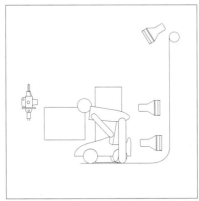

Side View

THE POWER OF DRIVING

▼

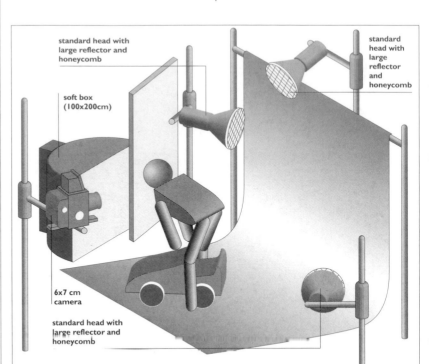

standard head with
large reflector and
honeycomb

standard
head with
large
reflector
and
honeycomb

soft box
(100x200cm)

6x7 cm
camera

standard head with
large reflector and
honeycomb

G LAMOUR PHOTOGRAPHY CAN ALSO EMBODY HUMOUR AND SOCIAL COMMENT.
AS GIANCARLO MECARELLI CONSISTENTLY DEMONSTRATES, IT CAN PROVIDE A MEANS OF
VISUALIZING SUBJECTS WHICH AT FIRST SIGHT HARDLY LEND THEMSELVES TO A GLAMOUR
TREATMENT — READ THE "PHOTOGRAPHER'S COMMENT" BELOW!

In a shot of this type, it is all too easy for the execution to fall short of the concept. You need the right model, the right expression, the right outfit, the right toy car, and, of course, the right lighting — all of which are manifestly present here.

The main light is a 100x200cm soft box some 2 metres from the model, to camera left; a large screen or flag protects the paper background from spill. Another light, 2 metres above the model, puts a little extra light onto her back which would otherwise be rather too dark. Two more lights throw discrete pools of light on the background, increasing the differentiation of the car from it. With the exception of the soft box, all the other lights are honeycombed for a more directional light.

Photographer's comment:

This shows the aggressiveness of motorists, and the foolishness of driving in Italy at all!

Photographer: **Rayment Kirby**

Client: **Own picture library**

Use: **Calendar**

Model: **Michelle**

Camera: **6x7 cm**

Lens: **180mm**

Exposure: **1/30 second at f/8**

Lighting: **Daylight plus reflector**

Film: **Fuji RDP 100**

Props & set: **Dressing table, etc., plus grasses and flowers.**

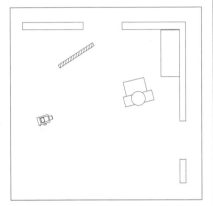

Plan View

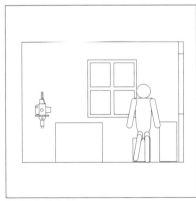

Side View

GIRL AT DRESSING TABLE

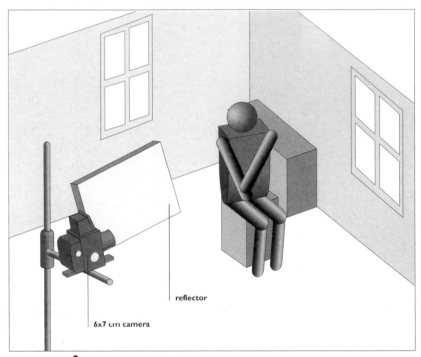

reflector

6x7 cm camera

Sᴏᴍᴇ ᴘʜᴏᴛᴏɢʀᴀᴘʜᴇʀs ᴛʀᴇᴀᴛ ᴛʜᴇɪʀ ʜᴏᴜsᴇs ᴀs ᴀ sᴇʀɪᴇs ᴏꜰ sᴇᴛs, ᴀɴᴅ ɪɴᴅᴇᴇᴅ ɪᴛ ɪs ɴᴏᴛ ᴜɴᴋɴᴏᴡɴ ꜰᴏʀ ᴛʜᴇᴍ ᴛᴏ ᴍᴏᴅɪꜰʏ ᴛʜᴇᴍ ꜰᴏʀ ᴛʜᴇ ᴘᴜʀᴘᴏsᴇs ᴏꜰ ᴘʜᴏᴛᴏɢʀᴀᴘʜʏ ᴀs ᴡᴇʟʟ ᴀs ꜰᴜʀɴɪsʜɪɴɢ ᴛʜᴇᴍ ᴀᴘᴘʀᴏᴘʀɪᴀᴛᴇʟʏ. Rᴀʏᴍᴇɴᴛ Kɪʀʙʏ's ᴏʟᴅ ꜰᴀʀᴍ ʜᴏᴜsᴇ ʜᴀs ᴍᴀɴʏ ᴘʜᴏᴛᴏɢʀᴀᴘʜɪᴄ sᴇᴛᴛɪɴɢs ɪɴsɪᴅᴇ ᴀɴᴅ ᴏᴜᴛ.

The lighting is very soft, with no true key; rather, the model is surrounded with light, from a window behind her and to camera right, and another larger window to camera left. A large reflector to camera left evens out the light somewhat for a very natural effect. Careful choice of props, and very harmonious colours relieved by the bright cosmetic jars, still further add to the sense of naturalness.

Despite the model's state of undress, this is in some ways a very innocent picture; there is a degree of voyeurism to it, in the sense that it purports to be a girl in her bedroom, but the model is clearly aware of the camera so that there is a sense of easy intimacy. She is a fantasy, but a harmless and indeed a seemingly attainable one.

Photographer's comment:

Available light from windows plus reflectors.

Photographer: **Rayment Kirby**

Client: **Own picture library**

Use: **Calendar**

Model: **Nikki**

Camera: **6x7 cm**

Lens: **180mm**

Exposure: **f/11**

Lighting: **Electronic flash: 1 head (soft box)
plus large white reflector "bounce".**

Film: **Kodak Ektachrome EPN**

Props & set: **Bowl, ewer and towel. Painted
paper background.**

Plan View

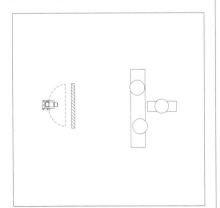

Side View

▼

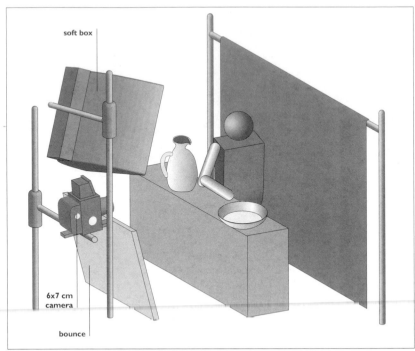

soft box

6x7 cm
camera

bounce

Dᴇᴄᴇᴘᴛɪᴠᴇʟʏ sɪᴍᴘʟᴇ ɪɴ ᴇᴠᴇʀʏ ᴡᴀʏ — ᴘʀᴏᴘs, ʙᴀᴄᴋɢʀᴏᴜɴᴅ, ᴄᴏᴍᴘᴏsɪᴛɪᴏɴ ᴀɴᴅ ʟɪɢʜᴛɪɴɢ —
ᴛʜɪs ᴘɪᴄᴛᴜʀᴇ sʜᴏᴡs (ᴀs ᴅᴏ sᴏ ᴍᴀɴʏ ᴏᴛʜᴇʀs ɪɴ ᴛʜɪs ʙᴏᴏᴋ) ᴛʜᴀᴛ ᴛʜᴇʀᴇ ɪs ɴᴏ sᴜʙsᴛɪᴛᴜᴛᴇ
ꜰᴏʀ ᴀ ɢᴏᴏᴅ "ᴇʏᴇ". Iᴛ ɪs ɪɴsᴛʀᴜᴄᴛɪᴠᴇ ᴛᴏ ᴀɴᴀʟʏᴢᴇ ɪᴛ ᴄᴀʀᴇꜰᴜʟʟʏ.

The ewer and basin clearly evoke a bygone atmosphere, but the shape of the ewer is curiously voluptuous in its own right. The yellow towel would have probably shocked our Victorian ancestors – white was the only colour for linen – yet a traditional white towel would have been too harsh; and besides, yellow emphasizes the almost sepia-tonality of the picture, as well as bouncing a skin-warming yellow onto the model and the wash-set. The triangular composition is simple and satisfying, and draws attention to the model's face with its cryptic half-smile. Finally, the background is unobtrusive, yet appropriate.

The lighting is no more than 750ws soft box above the camera, with a big white fill below it: the camera shoots through the gap between the two for very soft, even frontal lighting.

Photographer's comment:

Simple use of props to create atmosphere.

PHONE HOME

▼

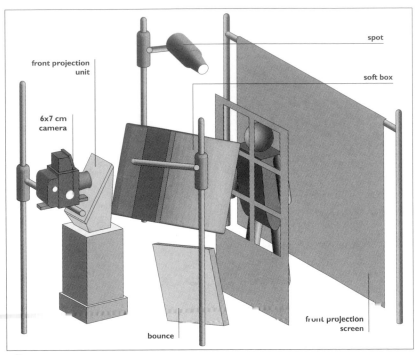

As with his picture on page 111, Rayment Kirby demonstrates how to integrate front projection with a real set: the cow parsley behind the right-hand panels of the door is real, and gives a three-dimensionality and reality to the background which would be lacking if it were only projected.

The key light is a 750ws soft box to camera right, with a louvred light restrictor/director, while a 400ws rim light picks up the model's hair and differentiates it from the background.

This is a fantasy, but not a cruel or exploitive one; the idea of a pretty but provocatively dressed (or undressed) girl at one's door would appeal to most men.

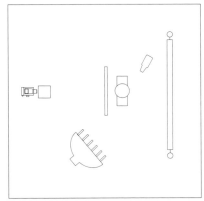

Plan View

Photographer: **Rayment Kirby** Client: **Own picture library** Use: **Calendar** Model: **Karen** Camera: **6x7 cm** Lens: **180mm** Exposure: **f/8** Lighting: **Electronic flash: 2 heads. Soft box and rim spot.** Film: **Kodak Ektachrome EPN 100** Props & set: **Red door; cow parsley; front projection of sunset for background.**

Photographer's comment:

A blend of reality and fantasy using front projection.

Photographer: **Peter Barry**

Client: **Model test**

Model: **Shelly**

Camera: **6x6 cm**

Lens: **80mm with Kodak Wratten 81C warming filter**

Exposure: **f/11**

Lighting: **Electronic flash: 1 head (soft box).**

Film: **Kodak Ektachrome 64**

Props & set: **Venetian mask. Background is hand-painted canvas.**

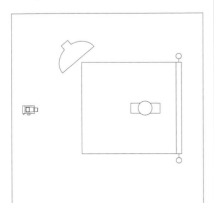

Plan View

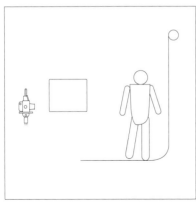

Side View

▼

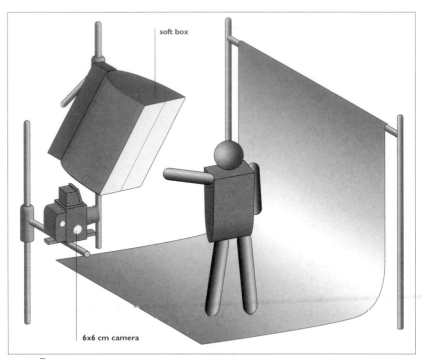

soft box

6x6 cm camera

The reflectivity of the golden Venetian mask determined the lighting in this shot; it had to be lit from the side, or it would have flared back at the camera and burnt out the highlights, even with slight underexposure.

The only light is a large soft box to camera left; there is no fill, and indeed the relatively dark background acts almost as a black bounce to absorb light. This strong directionality of light has several effects. One is to add to the mystery of the picture; it has connotations of night and secret assignations and aristocratic debaucheries. Another is to make it very graphic: the clear lines of the right side of the model's body and her right arm (both camera left, of course) draw still more attention to the mask. Yet a third is to make it simultaneously revealing (of the model's breasts) and modest (for those markets where pubic hair is *verboten*). The tip-toe pose emphasizes the firmness of the model's body, and makes her legs look even longer.

Photographer's comment:

I like the posed/theatrical feel of this shot.

Photographer: **Massimo Robecchi**

Assistant: **Teresa La Grotteria**

Client: **Studio magazine**

Use: **Editorial on hairstyling**

Model: **Roberta Griffa**

Make-up & hair: **Gianluca Rolandi**

Art director: **Vicky Sinaidis**

Camera: **35 mm SLR**

Lens: **180mm**

Exposure: **f/16**

Lighting: **Electronic flash: single soft box 140 x 200 cm, plus reflector panels.**

Film: **Konica Infrared b/w printed on Agfa Brovira**

Props & set: **White fabric background**

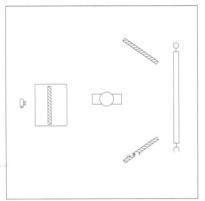

Plan View

Side View

▼

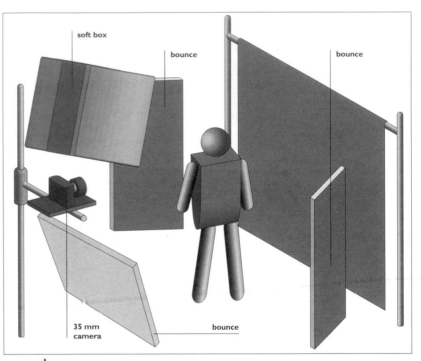

soft box

bounce

bounce

35 mm camera

bounce

Infrared film is fascinating stuff, but tricky to use effectively: it can result in a ghastly corpse-like pallor, which has to be countered with subtle gradations of tone and lighting which gives a well rounded form, as here.

The only light in this high-key set-up is a large soft box above and in front of the model, though a mirror directly below the soft box to reflect light back up at the model functions in effect as a second soft box about a stop down from the key. It is often more useful to think of mirrors as additional lights, rather than as reflectors. They are so directional and light losses can be calculated using the inverse square law. If you have a key light 2 metres from the subject, and a mirror which is also 2 metres from the subject but 1 metre from the key, the lighting ratio is 4:9 (2^2:3^2). In this case, there are also reflectors on either side of the model to even out the lighting still more.

Photographer's comment:

This girl is actually black, and it was hard to separate the hair tones from the skin tones; but with infrared film, her skin comes out white.

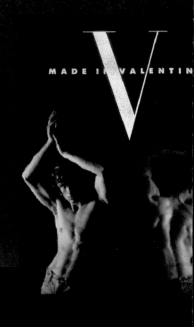

MADE IN VALENTIN

V

6

men and

groups

Little needs to be said about the male glamour picture, except perhaps to note that there may yet be a commercial future in a male equivalent of the "make-over" studio: a place where men can go to be photographed as cattle-drovers, rock stars, Harley riders, fashion models or whatever. Why should men not be able to realize fantasies of glamour in the same way as women? To some extent, the "old-time photo studios" cater to this need, allowing their clients to dress up as gangsters or cowboys, and maybe there is a place for developing this theme.

As for groups, creating a glamorous image of two or more people is even more difficult than glamourizing individuals. This is true whether the group in question is a couple, a family or (as in one picture in this chapter) three women in rather vintage-looking swimming outfits. The techniques required are perhaps closest to those of the glamour portrait, emphasizing the glamorous side of life without losing sight of reality, though there is also room (with the right models) for frank eroticism. The main difficulty lies in unifying the composition, so that the models are neither self-conscious, nor too distanced from one another; it is therefore worth paying particular attention to the posing in the group shots of this chapter.

▼

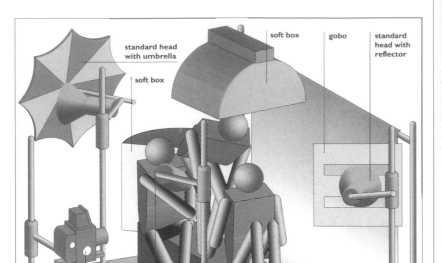

Ⓒoмpare this with "OUTBACK" on pages 128 and 129. Once

AGAIN, THE AIM IS TO SELL PAINTED BACKGROUNDS, AND HIGHLY DIRECTIONAL ELECTRONIC

FLASH LIGHTING HAS BEEN USED TO STREAK THE BACKGROUND IN ORDER

TO CREATE A RICH, VINTAGE AMBIANCE.

The key light on the girls is a flash head with a honeycomb to create a spot effect, with fill from two 120x120cm soft boxes and an umbrella flash. The background is lit with a single reflector head shining through a gobo consisting of a sheet of foam-core with two strips cut out of it to create the streaks.

Plan View

Photographer: **Jim DiVitale** Client: **Rear Window Backgrounds, Inc.** Use: **Brochure for painted backdrops** Models: **April Bundy, Nicole Griffin, Sue Gibson all from L'Agence** Make-up & hair: **Lisa Saul** Art directors: **Jon Weaver and Diego Sans** Camera: **6x6 cm** Lens: **150mm** Exposure: **f/11** Lighting: **Electronic flash: 5 heads.** Film: **Kodak Ektachrome 64** Props & set: **Two painted backdrops.**

Photographer's comment:

This image is now a permanent part of the Professional Photographers' of America (PPA) Travelling Loan Collection.

Photographer: **Giancarlo Mecarelli**

Client: **Personal work**

Models: **Patrizia Marcacci and Paolo**

Camera: **6x7 cm**

Lens: **180mm**

Exposure: **1/2 second at f/11**

Lighting: **Electronic flash (3 heads) and neon**

Film: **Kodak Ektachrome Panther 100 PRP**

Props & set: **Neon tube, paper background**

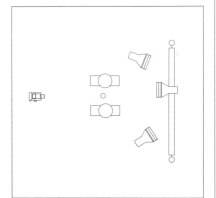

Plan View

Side View

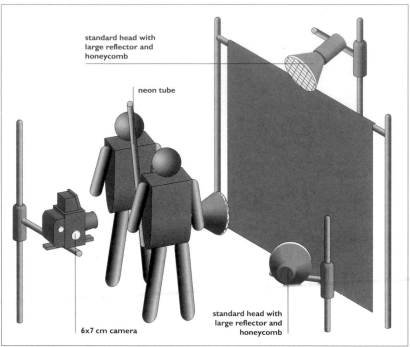

standard head with
large reflector and
honeycomb

neon tube

6x7 cm camera

standard head with
large reflector and
honeycomb

AIDS AND GLAMOUR? OUCH! BUT AS GIANCARLO MECARALLI REPEATEDLY DEMONSTRATES, THERE ARE VERY FEW SUBJECTS TO WHICH THE TECHNIQUES OF GLAMOUR PHOTOGRAPHY CANNOT BE APPLIED. YOU COULD HOWEVER CALL THIS "ANTI-GLAMOUR", WHICH USES THE CONVENTIONS OF GLAMOUR TO GO BEYOND GLAMOUR.

Some of the work in this book is commercial; some was shot speculatively; and there is some personal and portfolio work. The editorial aim was to strike a balance which showed not only what had been done (the commercial and speculative work) but also what could be done. Personal work is almost by definition the forerunner of the photographer's future commercial assignments. Compare this with the same photographer's "NEON AND KODAK" on pages 106 and 107, which is a conventionally commercial shot; and then consider how the photographer's mind worked, as he saw the red neon on his focusing screen. The lighting is clear enough from the diagram: two lights on the background echoing the silhouette of the couple, a back light to give the girl some identity, and the demonic glow of the red neon which separates the two.

Photographer's comment:

The burning question for me was how to make a picture out of this subject.

Photographer: **Dale Durfee**

Client: **Personal Work**

Use: **Exhibition**

Camera: **35 mm**

Lens: **100mm**

Exposure: **f/8**

Lighting: **Electronic flash: 2 heads. Soft box, 1 other head, and reflector.**

Film: **Polaroid Polapan**

Props & set: **Sheets, bed, pillows — all white.**

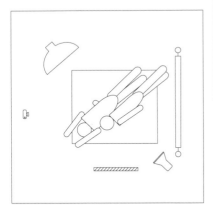

Plan View

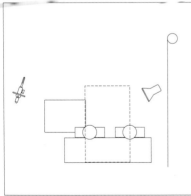

Side View

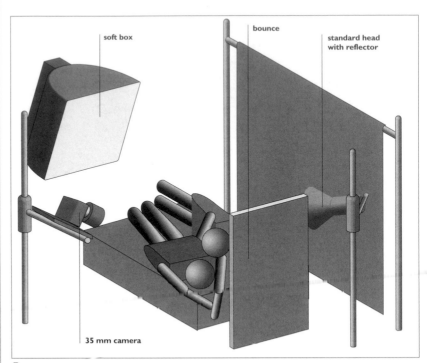

soft box

bounce

standard head with reflector

35 mm camera

DALE DURFEE'S ADVERTISING WORK IS WHAT SUPPORTS HER, BUT SHE GETS A GREAT DEAL OF IT ON THE STRENGTH OF HER PERSONAL WORK; THE SORT OF THING WHERE PEOPLE SAY, "OH, WE COULDN'T REALLY USE THAT — BUT COULD YOU DO SOMETHING IN THAT STYLE?"

The textures in this photograph are very important, and the classic way to get good texture is to use strongly angled lighting. On the other hand, too much chiaroscuro would remove the open, light, airy feel of the shot, a mood which is accentuated by the whiteness of the sheets. The lighting is therefore very glancing, but the shadows are well filled with both a soft box and a reflector in order to restrict the lighting range. The tonal range is of course very wide, from the pure white highlights of the sheets to the colour of the man's hair. It is interesting how the pose and the lighting interact — deeper shadows and stronger contrast might remove the essential honesty and innocence of the picture, and make it look clandestine.

Photographer's comment:

I wanted to convey a feeling of passion between two models who had never worked together before.

Photographer: **Dale Durfee**

Client: **Personal work**

Camera: **35 mm**

Lens: **105mm**

Exposure: **f/8**

Lighting: **Electronic flash: I head**

Film: **Ilford Delta 100**

Props & set: **Snake borrowed from pet shop:**
background painted half black, half white.

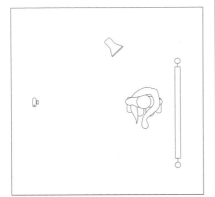

Plan View

Side View

▼

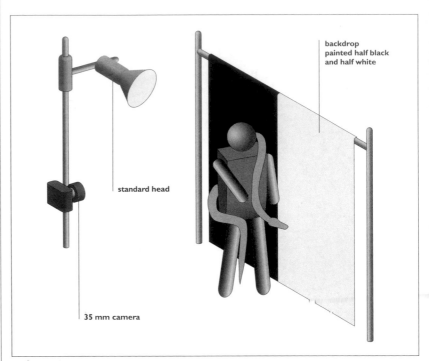

backdrop
painted half black
and half white

standard head

35 mm camera

LIKE SO MANY OF DALE DURFEE'S PICTURES, THIS IS ENDLESSLY MULTI-LAYERED: YOU CAN CEASELESSLY ANALYSE THE SYMBOLISM, AND THE REFERENCES, AND THE TONAL BALANCE AND SO FORTH. AND AGAIN LIKE SO MANY OF HER PICTURES, THERE IS ABSOLUTELY NO NEED TO DO SO: SHE HAS DONE THE WORK, SO YOU CAN JUST ENJOY THE PICTURE.

The preparations were simple enough: the wall was painted half black and half white. A model was found (and warned!), and the snake, all eight feet of reticulated python, was borrowed from a nearby pet shop.

The lighting could hardly have been simpler, either: a single L35 standard head to camera left, to give a hard, dramatic light. The picture was shot early in the session, as they were still learning how the snake behaved and how it crawled. Suddenly, the shapes and the shadows were perfect, and Dale shot the picture. She used 35 mm for speed and fluidity of action, but cropped to a square format to emphasize the dichotomy of black and white as single areas; otherwise, the model's legs and the background would have broken up the areas of tone.

EL TRIANGULO

▼

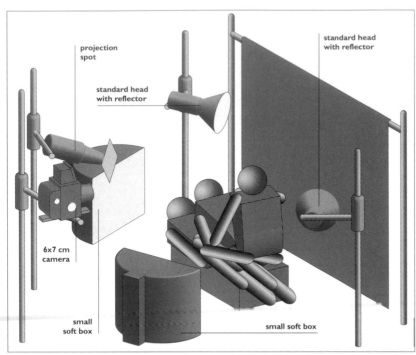

THIS IS A DELIGHTFULLY PLAYFUL PICTURE, IN WHICH THE REAL CHALLENGE LAY
IN CAPTURING THE BEAUTIFULLY GRADED SKIN TONES FROM THE VERY DARK-SKINNED MAN
THROUGH THE CHILD WITH SKIN LIKE DARK HONEY TO THE WOMAN WITH A CAUCASIAN
COMPLEXION. THE POSE IS ALSO NEATLY EXECUTED.

Effectively, the key light is the focusing spot to camera left. It delivers the same exposure as the diffused principal lights on either side of the camera (f/22) but creates the shadows and highlights because of its extra directionality. The background is lit a stop brighter than the principal subject (f/32) for a high-key effect, but not absolutely evenly, so there is some gradation in the background.

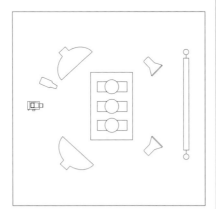

Plan View

Photographer: **Judith Vizcarra Puig** Client/Models: **Familia Font** Use: **Personal work** Make-up: **Silvia**
Camera: **6x7 cm** Lens: **180mm** Exposure: **f/22 or f/16** Lighting: **Electronic flash — 5 heads including 1
focusing spot** Film: **Fuji** Props & set: **Posing block, white paper background.**

Photographer's comment:

What is important in this picture is the triangular composition and the range of the skin tones.

Photographer: **Jordi Morgadas**

Client: *Penthouse* magazine

Use: **Editorial**

Camera: **35 mm**

Lens: **85mm with A-1 warming filter**

Exposure: **f/16**

Lighting: **Electronic flash: 2 heads. Soft box 100x200cm and spotlight.**

Film: **Kodak Ektachrome EPR 64**

Props & set: **Bedroom set**

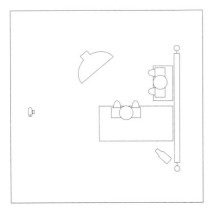

Plan View

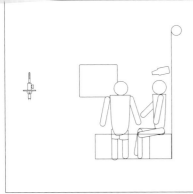

Side View

▼

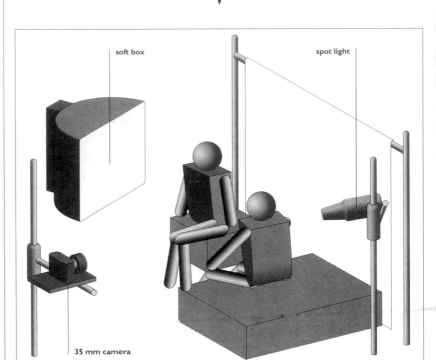

soft box   spot light

35 mm camera

Often, picture sets for men's magazines are shot outdoors or on location using mostly, or exclusively, available light, which is why so few shots of this type are to be found in this book. This example from Jordi Morgadas however, is shot with electronic flash.

The key light, a spot to the right of the camera, creates slight back lighting, illuminating in particular the luxurious blonde hair of the model on the right. This light is set fairly close to the ground, as if from a window. The fill is a 100x200 cm soft box to the left of the camera, set above the girls. The lighting ratio, measured with a flat-screen incident light meter, is just 2:1.

Low lighting ratios like these are quite commonplace in glamour photography for men's magazines, as they allow the richness of colour to be quite considerable. Slight underexposure, anything up to about half a stop, makes the skin tones in particular look very sensuous; but if the lighting ratio were any higher, then the shadows might well start to go very flat and dark.

Photographer's comment:

The aim was to create an atmosphere of intimacy between the two girls.

THE EMBRACE

▼

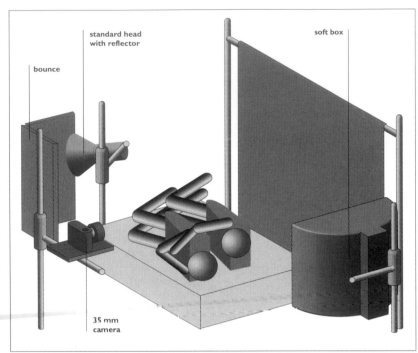

standard head
with reflector

bounce

soft box

35 mm
camera

Photographer: **Dale Durfee**

Client: **Self-promotional work for exhibition**

Camera: **35 mm**

Lens: **100mm**

Exposure: **f/8-1/2 (=f/9.5)**

Lighting: **Electronic flash: 2 heads. 1 soft box, 1 bounced head, with black flag to deepen shadows.**

Film: **Polaroid Polapan**

Props & set: **Shot on the studio floor**

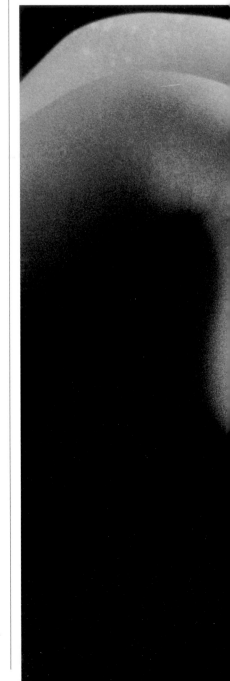

Compare this picture with the one on page 127. Both are of couples, but instead of passion in a light, airy setting, there is a quiet, loving embrace in moody, directional lighting, and the background is bare wood. The lightings and backgrounds could hardly be interchanged.

The lighting is essentially bi-directional. The key light comes from a single flash head to camera left, bounced from a reflector built from poly board, which illuminates the front of the couple. Then there is a soft box on the other side of the couple, slightly behind them, to the right of the camera. Directly opposite the camera, a black poly board kills shadows, making the dark areas really dark and moody.

In many glamour shots, texture is an essential part of the image. The tonality and grain of Polapan superimposes itself on the actual texture of the subjects and background, at once unifying them and providing a dreamy, slightly other-worldly dimension to the picture. The effect is somehow reminiscent of how one perceives the world when one is on the brink of sleep.

Photographer's comment:

I wanted to make the bodies fit together to convey a sense of security and warmth with the help of the light.

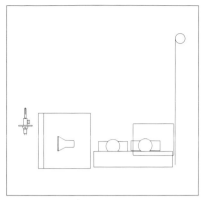

Side View

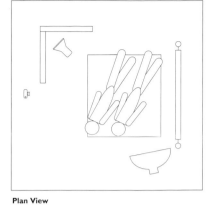

Plan View

Photographer: **Salvio Parisi**

Client: **Istituto Europeo di Design**

Use: **Jeans wear advertisement**

Model: **Luca Zecca**

Make-up & hair: **Anna Alliata**

Art director: **Adriano Caramenti**

Camera: **4x5 inch**

Lens: **300mm**

Exposure: **f/11 for electronic flash; 1/60 at f/8-1/2 (=f/9.5) for tungsten**

Lighting: **Soft box; with flash for 1 shot, with modelling light only for the other shot.**

Film: **Kodak Ektachrome 64D for tungsten shot. Kodak Ektachrome 64T for flash shot**

Props & set: **Black velvet background**

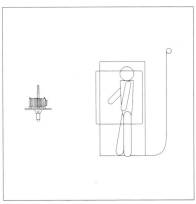

Plan View

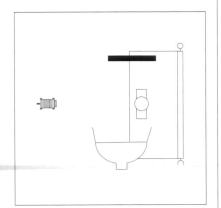

Side View

M A D E   I N   V A L E N T I N O

▼

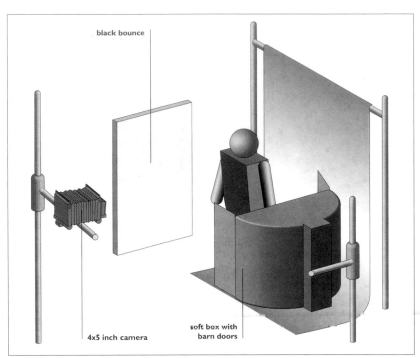

black bounce

4x5 inch camera

soft box with barn doors

THE SAME LIGHTING SET-UP WAS USED TO MAKE TWO EXPOSURES, ONE BY TUNGSTEN, ONE BY FLASH, BUT IN EACH CASE, THE "WRONG" FILM WAS USED. THE FINAL IMAGE CONSISTED OF TWO SHOTS DUPED TOGETHER UNDER TEXTURED GLASS, PLUS A LITH OF THE LOGO.

Each step in this picture is simple, but the way in which the whole idea is put together is very clever indeed. The lighting set up was a large soft box with barn doors to keep the light on the model. A black panel on the far side of the model reduced reflections and increased shadows. By shooting on the "wrong" films, the result was one very cold, blue image (electronic flash on tungsten balance film) and one very warm, yellow image (tungsten light on daylight balance film). The left-hand (blue) image was flopped (laterally reversed) for symmetry, while the two images were duplicated together through textured glass. Then an additional exposure of the lith logo added the big V and "Made in Valentino". Simple? Yes — once you know how to do it!

Photographer's comment:

The important thing is the use of two different films, duplicated together to create a unique effect.

MADE IN VALENTINO

7
glamour
elaborated

Few categories are ever watertight, and several of the pictures in this last chapter could possibly be re-assigned to Glamour Portraits (Chapter 1) or Fantasy (Chapter 7). There is however something which sets them aside from either category: a sort of self-referential quality, which deliberately takes our preconceptions and either turns them upside down or slyly reinforces them. Where it is present, the eroticism is rarely of the conventional type: instead, such moods and epochs are evoked as the Belle Epoque in Paris, the decadence of Berlin in the early 1930s or a "hippie chick" in the London of the 1960s. Again, there may also be some use of humour: the link between humour and glamour is all too often neglected. Most people look better when they, or we, are laughing or smiling; and the whole world is, in the strictest sense of the word, glamourized.

However all of the pictures in this chapter are unified by their exquisite attention to detail, which is necessary to create the mood that the photographer wanted. There is a kind of seamless quality: a sense of everything in the picture tending

Photographer: **Michael Barrington-Martin**

Use: **Advertisement**

Camera: **8x10 inch**

Lens: **360mm**

Exposure: **not recorded**

Lighting: **Electronic flash: soft box with small reflector for jewellery and black baffle to reduce fill-in on body.**

Film: **Agfachrome**

Props & set: **Seamless background**

Plan View

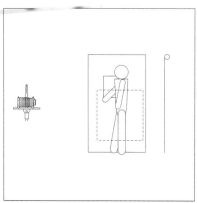

Side View

J E W E L L E R Y

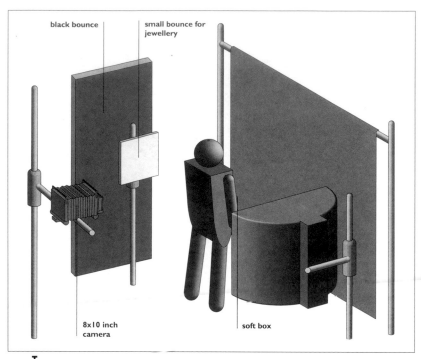

black bounce

small bounce for jewellery

8x10 inch camera

soft box

THIS WAS AN ADVERTISEMENT FOR COSTUME JEWELLERY. LIGHTING WAS VERY SIMPLE: A SINGLE 2000WS SOFT BOX. THE USE OF AN 8X10 INCH CAMERA IS WHAT EXPLAINS THE MAGICAL EFFECTS OF "SEEING INTO THE SHADOWS" — THE KIND OF DEFINITION WHICH IS SIMPLY UNATTAINABLE WITH SMALLER FORMATS.

Although modern films and selected lenses are very sharp indeed, allowing full-page reproductions from 6x7cm and even from smaller images, there is still a certain magic to 8x10inch originals which cannot be reproduced with smaller formats. Michael Barrington-Martin is an acknowledged master of seriously large format glamour photography, and of many other forms of large format work for that matter.

Here, the lighting was very simple indeed: a single soft box, with just one small reflector to kick some extra light into the jewellery. Overall, there was a large light-absorbing screen or flag to the model's right (camera left) to prevent excessive fill-in; and yet, you can see detail in the shadows which would barely be there in 4x5 inch and which would not be there at all in roll-film formats.

Photographer's comment:

This chick was very keen on me at the time and the session was most enjoyable. The client liked the shot, AND paid quickly.

PLAYER PIANO

▼

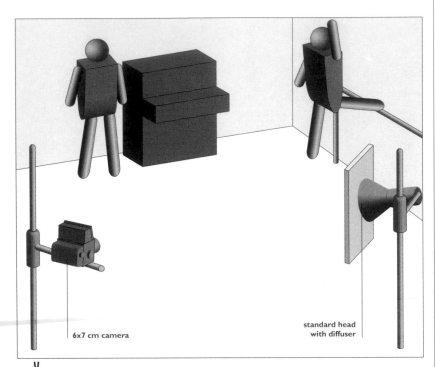

6x7 cm camera

standard head
with diffuser

Photographer: **Kenichi Ura**

Client: **YAMAHA**

Use: **Catalogue**

Hair: **Hamako Inatomi**

Art director: **Hideo Kasahara**

Camera: **6x7 cm**

Lens: **90mm**

Exposure: **1/4 second at f/11**

Lighting: **Electronic flash (1 head 1200ws) plus available light**

Film: **Kodak Ektachrome EPN**

Props & set: **Yamaha player piano on location**

Viewed dispassionately, this is a highly elaborate pack shot. The Yamaha self-playing piano is the product; the models and the studio are merely supporting props. Nevertheless, the picture is essentially glamorous, as it must be to sell a product which is not exactly essential to support life.

The principal lighting in this rather elaborate set is the daylight which comes from the windows high in the dance studio. Although this is perfectly adequate for the dancers, it is however too contrasty for colour film, which requires a much shorter contrast range. A 1200ws flash, diffused through tracing paper and bounced off the wall to the left of the camera, evened out the lighting ratio and created the illusion of natural light without the contrast. Technically speaking, the whole shot is somewhat overexposed, especially towards the top which has begin to flare; but aesthetically, this is absolutely correct for re-creating the mood and feel of a bright, airy dance studio. The overall impression is almost voyeuristic; so intense is the impression, one can very nearly smell the interior of the studio.

Photographer's comment:

The location is important. I wanted to express the pleasure an automatic self-playing piano can bring.

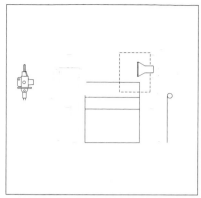

Side View

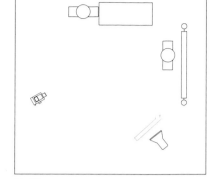

Plan View

Photographer: **Marc Joye**

Client: **Brass Palm**

Use: **Brochure/poster**

Models: **Renaud and Catherine**

Make-up & hair: **Chris Lens**

Art directors: **Marc Joye and Ben**

Camera: **4x5 inch**

Lens: **150mm**

Exposure: **f/22**

Lighting: **Electronic flash: 6 heads. 2 soft boxes (110x150cm and 80x80cm), 2 normal reflectors, 1 spot, 1 small effects light.**

Film: **Kodak Ektachrome 100**

Props & set: **Location**

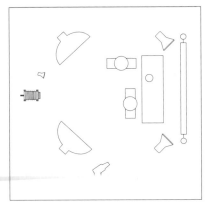

Plan View

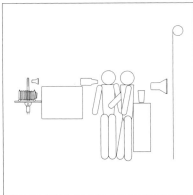

Side View

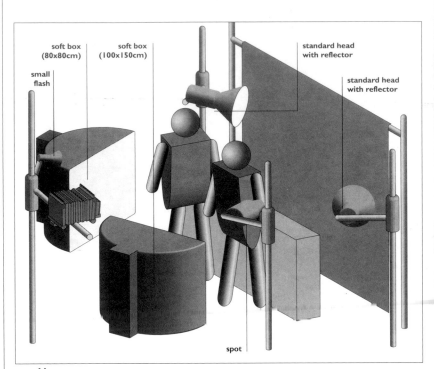

Mᴀʀᴄ Jᴏʏᴇ sᴜᴍs ɪᴛ ᴜᴘ ɪɴ ʜɪs ᴏᴡɴ ᴡᴏʀᴅs: ɪɴ ᴛᴇɴ ᴅᴀʏs, ʜᴇ ʜᴀᴅ ᴛᴏ ғɪɴᴅ ᴍᴏᴅᴇʟs, ʟᴏᴄᴀᴛɪᴏɴ, sᴛʏʟɪsᴛ, ᴍᴀᴋᴇ-ᴜᴘ ᴀɴᴅ ᴍᴏɴᴏᴄʟᴇ. Tʜᴇ ʙᴇᴇʀ ᴡᴀs ᴛʜᴇ ᴘʀᴏᴅᴜᴄᴛ ᴡʜɪᴄʜ ʜᴀᴅ ᴛᴏ ʙᴇ ʜɪɢʜʟɪɢʜᴛᴇᴅ, ᴀɴᴅ ɪᴛ ᴛᴏᴏᴋ ɴᴏ ғᴇᴡᴇʀ ᴛʜᴀɴ sɪx ʟɪɢʜᴛɪɴɢ ʜᴇᴀᴅs ᴛᴏ ɢᴇᴛ ɪᴛ ᴀʟʟ ᴛᴏɢᴇᴛʜᴇʀ.

The beer, of course, gets its own spotlight. But in addition to this, there is another low-powered effects light for the coat (which otherwise would have blocked up solid); two soft boxes to provide the overall light (look at the beer glass); and two lights for the background.

This is a good example of a lighting set-up which "just grew". The big 100x150cm soft light to camera right is the key, but the smaller 80x80cm soft light to camera left is also essential; The tonal range of the lighting would otherwise have been too great, let alone the tonal range of the subject. The spot for the beer is not direct; rather, it is reflected off the mirror behind the bar, and comes through the beer to give it its characteristic colour and sparkle. Then Guinness steals the copyline, "Pure Genius".

Photographer's comment:

The most difficult part was finding a monocle, or an optician able to make one. This was essential to the mood of the shot.

Photographer: **Philippe Merie**

Client: *Zeitgeist*

Use: **Editorial**

Model: **Louise Bjerring**

Make-up & hair: **Tromborg**

Camera: **35 mm**

Lens: **85mm**

Exposure: **1/60 second at f/4**

Lighting: **Tungsten: single head with fresnel.**

Film: **Kodak T-Max rated EI 1600-3200**

Props & set: **Armchair; wallpaper background.**

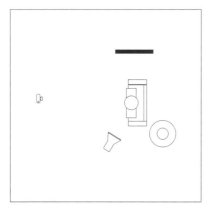

Plan View

Side View

LOUISE

▼

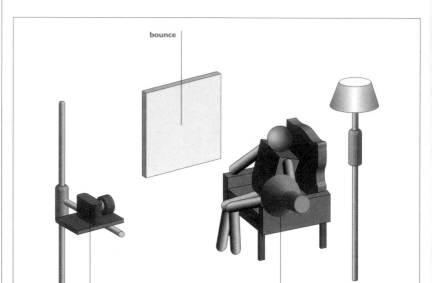

Simplicity is the keynote of this picture, as with so many others in the book. The only light is a single 250 watt tungsten head, with a fresnel lens. The tonality of the very fast film is exploited to give a tonal range which is at once soft and dramatic.

The single lamp was hand-held to camera right. The use of fast, grainy film in low and highly directional lighting creates a reportage feel which gives this picture a considerable degree of mystery. Who is this girl? Why is she dressed like this? She looks as if she is resting, or waiting: from what, or for what (or whom)? The cool directness of her stare at the camera bespeaks either enormous self-possession, or considerable world-weariness: which?

If it had been shot in colour, it would have been a very different picture, less reminiscent of the Paris of Doisneau or Brassaï, or the New York of Weegee the Famous; and the heavily textured, old-fashioned wallpaper conjures up even more the images of the old masters of photography.

Photographer's comment:

The important thing was to capture the mood.

Photographer: **Tom Bizzozzero**

Assistant: **Silvano Bricola**

Client: **Tubifer**

Model: **Micaela Vitale**

Make-up & hair: **Gianluca Rolandi**

Set decorator: **Gianni Maspero**

Use: **Advertising (poster)**

Camera: **4x5 inch**

Lens: **210mm**

Exposure: **f/8**

Lighting: **Electronic flash: 4 heads**

Film: **Kodak Ektachrome EPP 100**

Props & set: **Painted background, with table, phone, calculator and paper.**

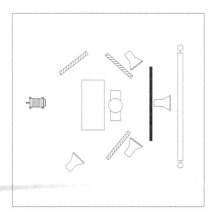

Plan View

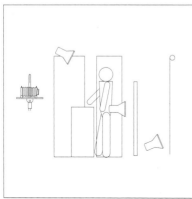

Side View

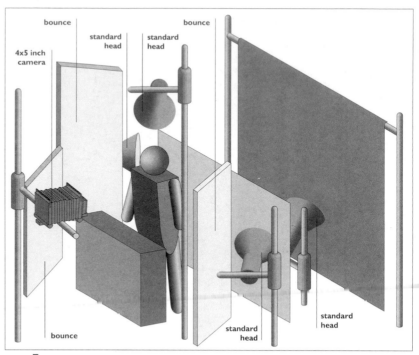

THIS IS CERTAINLY A FANTASY — BUT WHOSE? THE BOSS'S? THE SECRETARY'S? THE PHOTOGRAPHER'S? THE CLIENT'S? ONCE YOU HAVE THE CONCEPT, THE PROBLEM IS THE REALIZATION; AND THAT IS ENOUGH TO EXERCISE ANYONE. WITH FOUR HEADS, TWO BACKGROUNDS AND NO SOFT BOXES, THIS IS A DEMANDING LIGHTING SET.

Making things hang in mid-air is always a problem. You can do it the hard way, by throwing them in the air and using flash to freeze them before they fall; or you can exercise some ingenuity, by suspending or supporting them with wire. A solution borrowed from the movie industry is hair-fine tungsten wire, available from special effects suppliers, or you can hide the wire in the telephone cord as was done here.

The key light is to camera right, about 45 degrees to the camera/subject axis, with a reflector to camera left to fill the shadows. Then there are two more lights for the specially-constructed first background, and a fourth light for the blue sweep behind that background.

Photographer's comment:

Once we had agreed the concept, the problems lay in the technical difficulties of the flying phone and other suspended objects.

BMW Z1

▼

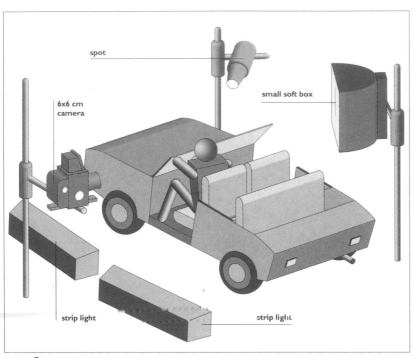

spot

small soft box

6x6 cm camera

strip light

strip light

Pretty girls have always been used to sell cars. This is part of a set for a BMW calendar showing BMW cars and motorcycles from the earliest models to the present — with a pretty girl, of course!

Strips, laid on the ground, were carefully arranged to give Z-shaped reflections to echo the car's name. A hair-light helped to "lift" the model's hair and differentiate it from the upholstery: a blonde model made this easier. A small soft box behind the car and to camera left gave adequate lighting of the dark upholstery and interior without over-lighting the model, which is a perennial problem in car photography.

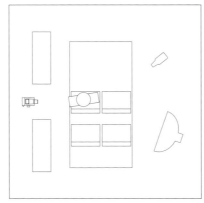

Plan View

Photographer: **Ron McMillan** Client: **L&C BMW** Use: **Calendar** Model: **Katie Orgill** Make-up & hair: **Dexi** Camera: **6x6 cm** Lens: **120mm with 81b filter** Exposure: **f/11** Lighting: **Electronic flash: 4 heads. 2 strips, 1 "fish fryer" small soft box, 1 hair light.** Film: **Fuji RDP ISO 100** Props & set: **BMW Z1; gravel on floor of cove to create impression of gravel drive.**

Photographer's comment:

It took ages to arrange the strip lights in order to get the Z-shaped reflections right. Most people notice this only subliminally if at all, but it is a nice touch.

Photographer: **Giancarlo Mecarelli**

Client: **L'Europeo**

Use: **Magazine cover story**

Model: **Alona G.**

Make-up & hair: **Agata Branchina**

Art director: **Giovanni Sammarco**

Stylist: **Max**

Camera: **6x7 cm**

Lens: **180mm**

Exposure: **f/22**

Lighting: Electronic flash: 3 heads, including 1 **soft box.**

Film: **Kodak Ektachrome Panther PRP ISO 100**

Props & set: **Paper background; specially made signs**

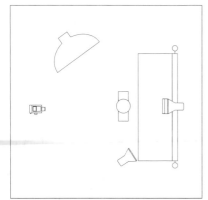

Plan View

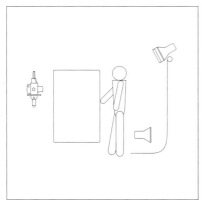

Side View

▼

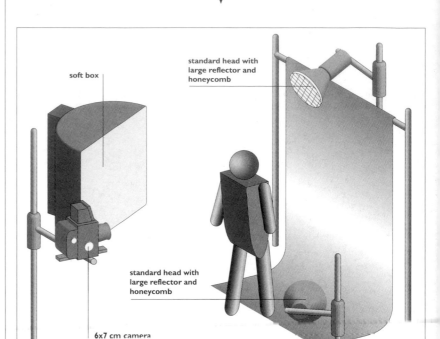

standard head with large reflector and honeycomb

soft box

standard head with large reflector and honeycomb

6x7 cm camera

Somehow, it was impossible to resist this as the last image in the book: STOP, GO NO FURTHER. If you have read the book from start to finish, you will recognize the style of Giancarlo Mecarelli, a combination of often bittersweet humour with exquisite technique.

The lighting set-up is straightforward: a soft box to camera left, at approximately 45 degrees to the camera/subject axis, supplemented by a hairlight (Evenlite with honeycomb) suspended above and behind the model. The background is lit separately with another Evenlite-plus-honeycomb: the plain blue paper of the background contrasts with the warmth of the model's skin and the bright red of the prohibition signs. If there is a single lesson to be gained from this whole book, it can be summed up as Occam's Razor: *"Entia non sunt multiplicanda praeter necessitatem"* — entities should not be multiplied without cause. The best lighting is the simplest lighting which will create the effect that you want; but if you have to use extra heads, reflectors, flags and so forth, you should be ready and willing to use them, and they should be available for you to use.

Photographer's comment:

The client asked me to take a picture symbolizing the new forms of social prohibition against smoking, eating, sex and so forth. . .

8
directory of

Photographer: **MICHAEL BARRINGTON-MARTIN**
Nationality: BRITISH
Address: OLD TIMBERS, BLACKWATER CORNER,
GRISTON, NEAR WATTON
NORFOLK IP25 6PT
ENGLAND
Telephone: + 44 (1 953) 88 48 41
Biography: *A photographer of considerable
experience, his work in nude
photography first brought him fame but
now he works in many other fields
including product shots and on location
for major clients.*
Glamour shot: Jewellery p140/141

Photographer: **PETER BARRY**
Nationality: BRITISH
Address: 57 FARRINGDON ROAD,
LONDON EC1M 3JB
ENGLAND
Telephone: + 44 (1 71) 430 0966
Fax: + 44 (1 71) 430 0903
Biography: *Peter Barry's work is extremely varied –
fashion, advertising, girls, still life and
food – and so every day is different,
exciting and stimulating. Constantly
learning and experimenting with new
techniques, his two main passions are
people and food. He has travelled all
over the world and met many
fascinating people and as a result he
feels that photography is not so much
work as a way of life.*
**Glamour shots: Girl in Teddy p96/97,
Homage to Vargas p100/101, Girl in
Canvas p102/103, Cheeky Girl
p104/105, Venetian Masked Nude
p116/117**

Photographer: **MARIO DI BENEDETTO**
Firm: WANTED
Nationality: ITALIAN
Address: VIA PEROSI 5
20146 MILANO
ITALY
Telephone: + 39 (2) 48 95 26 50
Fax/phone: + 39 (2) 42 34 898
Biography: *Advertising photographer since 1982;
in 1994 created "Wanted" studio,*

*working in advertising, still life, digital
photography, fashion, beauty, industry,
special projects.*
Glamour shot: Primavera p37/39

Photographer: **TOM BIZZOZZERO**
Firm: CAFÉ ESTUDIOS
Nationality: ITALIAN
Address: VIA GIOVANNI DA CERMENATE 23
22063 CANTÙ – COMO
ITALY
Telephone/Fax: + 39 (31) 71 66 82
Biography: *Born in 1947. A "fanatic" in
photography from the earliest age.
Began working professionally in 1967,
with black and white reportage in travel
and adventure. Specialized in
underwater pictures, but for the last few
years has worked exclusively in
advertising.*
Glamour shot: Secretary p148/149

Photographer: **SIMON CHIN**
Nationality: MALAYSIAN
Address: 165 JALAN AMINUDDIN BAKI
TAMAN TUN DRIVE
ISMAIL 60 000
KUALA LUMPUR
MALAYSIA
Telephone: + 60 (3) 718 8831
Fax: + 60 (3) 717 3736
Biography: *Simon Chin studied advertising
photography in the U.S. and later
worked there as a photographer's
assistant. Upon return to Malaysia he
started freelancing as a photographer
for two years before joining three other
photographers to open the studios
where he is presently located.*
Glamour shot: Mimi p26/7

Photographer: **BENNY DE GROVE**
Firm: FOTOSTUDIO DE GROVE BVBA
Nationality: BELGIAN
Address: ZWIJNAARDSESTEENWEG 28A
9820 MERELBEKE
BELGIUM
Telephone: + 32 (92) 31 96 16
Fax: + 32 (92) 31 95 94
Biography: *Studied photography at Academy of
Gent for 2 years; photographer since
1984; has had many posters and
postcards published worldwide. Works
mostly as illustration photographer and
for magazines and publicity agencies.
Work has appeared frequently in*

photo-magazines.
**Glamour shots: Prisoned Justice p54/55,
Back to the Beginning p62/63, Soon
My Sailor Will Come p94/95**

Photographer: **JAMES DiVITALE**
Firm: DIVITALE PHOTOGRAPHY
Nationality: AMERICAN
Address: 420 ARMOUR CIRCLE NE
ATLANTA
GA 30324
USA
(STUDIO)
PO BOX 95127
ATLANTA
GA 30347–0127
USA (MAILING)
Telephone: + 1 (404) 892 7973
Fax: + 1 (404) 938 1394
Biography: *Jim DiVitale has been a commercial
photographer specializing in people
and products in Atlanta for sixteen
years. Nine years ago, he established
his own studio together with his wife
Sandy, who acts as the studio's
production coordinator. Jim's work
has been recognized in annuals such
as Advertising Photographers of
America's Creative Awards (One and
Two); Graphis Photo 93 and 94; and
Professional Photographers of
America's Loan Collection 1990,
1992, 1993 and 1994. He has
published his work in the Creative
Black Book 1992–1995, Workbook
1995, Single Image Workbook
#15–18, Klik!/Showcase Photography
#2–4, and the Art Directors' Index
1995.*
**Glamour shot: Poolside Maneuvers
p122/123**

Photographer: **DALE DURFEE**
Nationality: AMERICAN WORKING IN LONDON
Address: UNIT 2
38 ST. OSWALDS PLACE
LONDON SE11 5JE
ENGLAND
Telephone: + 44 (1 71) 735 8766
Fax: + 44 (1 71) 582 5662
Biography: *Born in the U.S. Worked for Hallmark,
came to England on sabbatical, and
has worked here since 1979. Mainly*

advertising work.

Glamour shots: Bottoms Up p74/76, Regina 077/79, Passion p126/127, Man with Snake p128/129, The Embrace p134,135

Photographer: **MICHÈLE FRANCKEN**
Firm: N.V. FRANCKEN CPM
Nationality: BELGIAN
Address: VLAANDERENSTRAAT 51
9000 GENT
BELGIUM
Telephone: + 32 (9) 225 4308
Fax: + 32 (9) 224 2132
Biography: *Michèle Francken has worked since 1977 in a family business with her two brothers and four others. N.V. Francken CPM has its own colour laboratory and specializes in fashion catalogues and fabrics. Michèle experiments with personal work alongside her commercial work, and has also had several exhibitions.*

Glamour shots: Lingerie I p82/83, Lingerie II p84/85

Photographer: **AL HAMDAN**
Nationality: BRAZILIAN
Address: RUA BARÃO DO FLAMENGO 22
GRUPO 301
RIO DE JANEIRO
BRAZIL 22 220–080
Telephone: + 55 (21) 265 4047
Fax: + 55 (21) 225 5967
Biography: *Al Hamdan is an art photographer and advertising photographer, born in Rio de Janeiro. His main clients include Coca-Cola, MacDonald's, Xerox, IBM, Sousa Cruz (tobacco), De Millus (lingerie) and Fleischmann Royal (food); agencies for whom he has worked include McCann Erickson, DPZ, Contemporânea, VS, GR 3, Animus, Setembro, Umuarama and Salles. He has won a number of awards, stretching back to The Best in Advertising in the State of Minas Gerais (AMP) 1980; Photographer of the Year (ABP) 1984; and Best Studio – Premio Colunistas Produção Nacional 1991.*

Glamour shot: Lingerie p48/49

Photographer: **ANDREW GORDON HOBBS**
Nationality: NEW ZEALANDER
Address: UNIT 2
38 ST. OSWALDS PLACE
LONDON SE11 5JE
ENGLAND
Telephone: MOBILE (0956) 225776
Fax: + 44 (1 71) 253 3007
Biography: *Original interests were in cinematography, but owing to a lack of colleges in the area, he took up still photography instead. A good friend ran a model agency, and so he was never short of good models. Influences included Norman Parkinson and Helmut Newton, and he went first to Sydney and then to London, where after the initial culture shock he claims to have settled in quite well.*

Glamour shot: Glamour in Fashion p60/61

Photographer: **MARC JOYE**
Nationality: BELGIAN
Address: BRUSSELBAAN 262
1790 AFFLIGEM
BELGIUM
Telephone: + 32 (53) 662 945
Fax: + 32 (53) 662 952
Biography: *After graduating at H.R.I.T.C.S. in Brussels, he worked for a short while as a movie editor. Then he had the opportunity to get into the world of advertising photography, and in 1977 he started his own studio. Besides studio work, he likes shooting with his Sinar and Broncolor flash on location.*

Glamour shots: Samurai Women p40/41, 1900 p144/145

Photographer: **RAYMENT KIRBY**
Nationality: BRITISH
Address: COGGERS FARM, HORAM
HEATHFIELD
EAST SUSSEX TN21 0LT
ENGLAND
Telephone: + 44 (1 453) 812 148
Biography: *Began by working as a photographer in the R.A.F., and then in studios in London. He worked in advertising and magazines, and in the record industry. he wrote a book called* Photographing Glamour, *and is now based in Sussex where he runs a picture library and designs and manufactures large format cameras.*

Glamour shots: Girl at Window p90/91, Girl at Dressing Table p110/111,

Morning Toilette p112/113, Phone Home p114/115

Photographer: **PETER LAQUA**
Nationality: GERMAN
Address: MARBACHERSTR. 29
78048 VILLINGEN
GERMANY
Telephone: + 49 (7721) 30501
Fax: + 49 (7721) 30355
Biography: *Born in 1960, Peter Laqua studied portraiture and industrial photography for three years. Since 1990 he has had his own studio, specializing in industrial clients. A prizewinner in the 1994 Minolta Art Project, he has also had exhibitions on the theme of "Pol-Art" (fine art photography with Polaroid materials) in 1994 and on the theme of "Zwieback" in Stuttgart in 1992*

Glamour shot: Filmstar p22/23

Photographer: **RON McMILLAN**
Nationality: BRITISH
Address: THE OLD BARN
BLACK ROBINS FARM
GRANT'S LANE
EDENBRIDGE
KENT TN8 6QP
ENGLAND
Telephone: + 44 (1 732) 866 111
Fax: + 44 (1 732) 867 223
Biography: *Ron McMillan has been an advertising photographer for over 20 years. He recently custom built a new studio, converting a 200-year-old barn on a farm site on the Surrey/Kent borders. This rare opportunity to design a new drive-in studio from scratch allowed Ron to put all his experience to use in its layout, as well as providing a full range of facilities including a luxury fitted kitchen. Ron's work covers food, still life, people and travel, and over the years it has taken him to numerous locations in Europe, the Middle East and the U.S.*

Glamour shot: BMW Z1 p150/151

Photographer: **GIANCARLO MECARELLI**
Nationality: ITALIAN
Address: VIA BULLONA 10
20154 MILANO
ITALY
Telephone: + 39 (2) 34 75 85
Fax: + 39 (2) 83 78 580
Biography: *Giancarlo Mecarelli was born in Trevi (PG) in 1946 and studied in San Paolo, Brazil, where he began to work in the field of communications as an illustrator and later as an Art Director. Because the art of photography was his great passion, he later decided to become a professional photographer, believing that the most important thing was to have as personal a style in photography as he has in illustration. He has been living in Italy for eight years, and works as Art Director and Photographer in Strategia, an advertising monthly magazine, and for many news weeklies such as Panorama, L'Espresso, L'Europeo, etc.*
Glamour shots: Women in Tension p34/36, Coloured Paper p46/47, Neon and Kodak p106/107, The Power of Driving p108/109, HIV p124/125, Do Not Pass p152/153

Photographer: **PHILIPPE MERIE**
Nationality: DANISH
Address: NANSENSGADE 61C
1366 COPENHAGEN K
DENMARK
Telephone: + 45 (33) 11 18 54
Fax: + 45 (33) 14 38 54
Biography: *With a French father and a Norwegian mother, Philippe had an international upbringing and is now based in Copenhagen. He has been a professional photographer for 18 years: his clients include Ted Bates, McCann Erickson, Y&R, Saatchi & Saatchi and his editorial work has appeared in Café, Elle, In and other magazines.*
Glamour shot: Louise p146/147

Photographer: **RICKY LOKE SAI MING**
Firm: WE STUDIO SDN. BHD.
Nationality: MALAYSIAN
Address: 10 JALAN SS4D/14
47301 PETALING JAYA
SELANGOR DARUL EHSAN
MALAYSIA
Telephone: + 60 (3) 703 1899
Fax: + 60 (3) 703 6613
Biography: *He started his own studio in 1987, and the team at We Studio now consists of 15 people. They work in a broad range, including interiors, corporate brochures, annual reports and fashion, and travel internationally in order to keep up with and gain access to the latest technology.*
Glamour Shot: Carmen Creah p30/31

Photographer: **JORDI MORGADAS**
Nationality: SPANISH
Address I: DIPUTACIÓN 317
1º 08009 BARCELONA
SPAIN
Telephone: + 34 (3) 488 25 68
Fax: + 34 (3) 488 34 65
Address II: LOS NELESES S/N
22145 RADIQUERO
HUESCA
SPAIN
Telephone: + 34 (908) 83 25 35
Biography: *Born in April 1946. At 19, he decided to concentrate totally on photography. Self taught, like many of his generation, he found work in many fields from portaiture to industrial photography to magazine photography as a correspondent for the EFE agency. Later, his nude photography appeared in such magazines as Playboy, Penthouse and Interviù, including a number of cover pictures. Now, he works exclusively in advertising, specializing in beach wear, lingerie and nudes.*
Glamour shots: Flor y Mujer p42/43, Retrato de Nuria p58/59, Suave p66/67, Corseteria I p86/87, Corseteria II p88/89, Penthouse II p132/133

Photographer: **SALVIO PARISI**
Nationality: ITALIAN
Address I: VIA XX SETTEMBRE 127
20099 SESTO S.G.
MILANO
ITALY
Telephone: + 39 (2) 22 47 25 59 AND
+ 39 (2) 26 22 55 67
Fax: + 39 (2) 71 44 30
Address II: VIA MILISCOLA 31
80072 ARCO FELICE
NAPOLI
ITALY
Telephone: + 39 (81) 86 63 553
Fax: + 39 (81) 86 61 241
Biography: *The essentially commercial nature of his photography works things in such a way that in his images, people, models and objects become a purely physical support for the basic advertising idea or product. "Accessories" such as charm, styling, femininity and appeal are only apparently left out. That's how a "beautiful" face becomes the best basis for make-up; a sculptured leg, a way of showing off a shoe; and a detail of a body a complement to a perfume.*
Glamour shots: Angie p20-21, Made in Valentino p136/137

Photographer: **JUDITH VIZCARRA PUIG**
Nationality: SPANISH
Address: AV LLIBERTAT 31
MOLLET DE VALLES
08100 BARCELONA
SPAIN
Telephone: + 34 (3) 593 59 01
Biography: *Specializes in portraits, creative photography, and running practical photographic seminars.*
Glamour shots: Sola p64/5, El Triangulo p130/131

Photographer: **MASSIMO ROBECCHI**
Firm: CAFÉ ESTUDIOS
Nationality: ITALIAN
Address I: VIA MOREO 3
2201 LAGLIO (COMO)
ITALY
Telephone/Fax:+ 39 (31) 71 66 82
Address II: C/O REP: BETTINA MÜLLER
50 NEULERCHENFELDERSTRAßE
A–1160 WIEN
AUSTRIA
Telephone/Fax:+43 (1) 40 32 979
Biography: *Born in Milan in 1960, he started working as an assistant at a major*

studio in 1980, and now works equally happily in still life, fashion and beauty for editorial use and advertising campaigns. Important clients include Backer Spielvogel Bates, Chivas Regal, Fiat, Kim Top Line, Levis, Proctor & Gamble, Warner Bros and others. To improve his experience in other countries, he is interested in working with agents outside Italy.

Glamour shots: Butterfly p44/45, Nude 3 p72/73, Nude 1 p118/119

Photographer: **GÉRARD DE SAINT MAXENT**
Nationality: FRENCH
Address: 14 BD EXELMANS
75016 PARIS
FRANCE
Telephone: + 33 (1) 42 24 43 33
Biography: *Has worked in advertising and publicity since 1970. Specializes in black and white.*

Glamour shot: Pharmaceutical Advertisement p68/69

Photographer: **NIGEL SHUTTLEWORTH**
Nationality: BRITISH
Address: YEW HOUSE
ALLERY BANKS
MORPETH
NORTHUMBERLAND
NE61 2SW
ENGLAND
Telephone: + 44 (1 670) 51 80 01
Biography: *Nigel Shuttleworth is a freelance commercial photographer working in Northumberland, UK. In 1993/4 he held a one-man exhibition following a documentary project on the last deep mine and mining community in the north-east. He has had work published in the* Photography Yearbook *and the educational series* Cultures of World *following a commission to take photographs in Hungary and the Czech Republic.*

Glamour shot: Nude p70/71

Photographer: **ROBERT STEDMAN**
Nationality: AMERICAN (RESIDENT IN SINGAPORE)
Address: BLOCK 28
KALLANG PLACE #03–16/17
SINGAPORE 1233
Telephone: + 65 294 4101
Fax: + 65 294 0515
Biography: *Robert Stedman originally hails from Los Angeles, California. After graduating university he decided to seek adventure in the South Seas and signed aboard as first mate on a trading schooner. He finally ended up in South-East Asia where he worked for many years as a freelance photojournalist – travelling extensively in Asia, China, Central Europe, Africa and the U.S. In 1988, he established a photography and graphic design studio in Singapore which serves a wide range of local and multinational companies.*

Glamour shot: Subtle Seduction p24/5

Photographer: **RINGO TANG**
Firm: RINGO TANG PHOTO WORKSHOP
Nationality: HONG KONG
Address I: G/F 31 ROBINSON ROAD
HONG KONG
Telephone: + 852 521 5185
Fax: + 852 868 5456
Address II: MOVIOLA PRODUCTIONS LTD.
12 LI KWAN AVENUE, 1ST FLOOR
TAI HANG
HONG KONG
Telephone: + 852 577 1166
Fax: + 852 376 6677
Biography: *Ringo Tang, a Hong Kong native, has been a professional photographer since 1984. A self taught photographer, he has participated in numerous exhibitions in Hong Kong and internationally. He has won such awards as the Art Director's Club Choice Award of New York and the Communication Arts' Award of Excellence. In addition to being exhibited, Ringo's photographs have been published in a variety of publications including Graphis of Switzerland and Communication Arts of the U.S. Successfully established as one of Hong Kong's pre-eminent fashion photographers, Ringo has now also taken to directing television commercials.*

Glamour shots: Fiona Sproat p18/19, The Last Embrace p28/9

Photographer: **COLIN THOMAS**
Nationality: BRITISH
Address: 56 WHITFIELD STREET
LONDON W1P 5RN
ENGLAND
Telephone: + 44 (1 71) 637 4786
Fax: + 44 (1 71) 323 5512
Biography: *He has been working in professional photography since he left art college 20 years ago. He started as an assistant, and now has his own large West End studio with two assistants and all facilities. "It's been bloody hard work, but fun".*

Glamour shots: Golden Nude p52/53, Chaise Lingerie p92/93

Photographer: **KENICHI URA**
Firm: JIB Co.
Nationality: JAPANESE
Address: 7–4–7 HIGASHI–NAKAHAMA
JŌTO–KU
OSAKA
JAPAN
Telephone: + 81 (6) 968 5454
Fax: + 81 (6) 963 31720
Biography: *1945 Born in Osaka
1968 member of Hidano photographer office.
1971 freelance.
1987 established JIB Co.*

Glamour shot: Player Piano p142/143

Photographer: **GÜNTHER UTTENDORFER**
Nationality: GERMAN
Address: KRUMMENACKERSTRASSE 17–19
73733 ESSLINGEN
GERMANY
Telephone: + 49 (711) 35 66 88
Fax: + 349 (711) 350 83 37
Biography: *Age 31, self-employed since 1987. Mainly shooting fashion (especially lingerie and bathing suits). Studio is 250 sq. m. in an old factory. He used to shoot still life, but got awfully bored with it and is now working with people, which he finds much more fun.*

Glamour shot: Eva p50/51

Acknowledgements

First and foremost, we must thank all the photographers who gave so generously of pictures, information and time. We hope we have stayed faithful to your intentions, and we hope you like the book, despite the inevitable errors which will have crept in. It would be invidious to single out individuals, but it is an intriguing footnote that the best photographers were often the most relaxed, helpful and indeed enthusiastic about the Pro Lighting series.

We must also thank Christopher Bouladon and his colleagues in Switzerland, and of course Brian Morris who invented the whole idea for the series; and in Britain, we owe a particular debt to Colin Glanfield, who was the proverbial "ever present help in time of trouble."

The manufacturers and distributors who made equipment available for the lighting pictures at the beginning of the book deserve our thanks too: Photon Beard, Strobex and Linhof and Professional Sales (UK importers of Hensel flash). And finally, we would like to thank Chris Summers, whose willingness to make reference prints at odd hours made it much easier for us to keep track of the large numbers of pictures which inevitably crossed our desks.